COMMON SENSE, INTUITION, *AND* GOD'S GUIDANCE

C. Christopher Knippers, Ph.D.

THOMAS NELSON PUBLISHERS

NASHVILLE

Published in Nashville, Tennessee, by Thomas Nelson, Inc.

Scripture quotations are from the NEW KING JAMES VERSION of the Bible. Copyright © 1979, 1980, 1982, Thomas Nelson, Inc., Publishers.

Scripture quotations noted CEV are from the CONTEMPORARY ENGLISH VERSION. Copyright © 1991, American Bible Society.

Scripture quotations noted TLB are from *The Living Bible* (Wheaton, Illinois: Tyndale House Publishers, 1971) and are used by permission.

Library of Congress Cataloging-in-Publication Data

Knippers, C. Christopher.
    Common sense, intuition, and God's guidance / C. Christopher Knippers.
        p.   cm.
    Includes bibliographical references.
    ISBN 0-8407-3455-7 (pbk.)
    1. Health—Religious aspects—Christianity. 2. Common sense.
3. Christian life—1960– I. Title.
BT732.K65   1993
248.4—dc20   92-38695
                                                                    CIP

Printed in the United States of America

1 2 3 4 5 6 7 — 98 97 96 95 94 93

ACKNOWLEDGMENTS

God gave me the words of this book. I often sat down at the word processor not knowing what I was going to say, and the words just started flowing.

Greg Anderson, author of *The Cancer Conqueror* and *The Triumphant Patient*, believed in this book enough to call it to the attention of Ronald Haynes of Thomas Nelson Publishers, who also believed in it enough to make its publication possible.

Dr. Claire Riley helped me gain the higher level of communication with God that inspired the writing of this book.

There are many people who have believed in

me enough to encourage me to write about my experiences. Some to whom I am especially grateful are: Dr. Cecil and Eloise Knippers, Sue Udell, Cindy Hecker, Joe Lauderdale, and Rev. Robert A. Schuller and the congregation of his Rancho Capistrano Community Church. These people believed in me even when it was hard for me to believe in myself.

FOREWORD

In 1985 a handful of fellow cancer patients and I started a support group called Cancer Conquerors. We vowed to support each other through life-threatening illness by encouraging one another to mobilize our full resources against our diseases.

Soon we were visited by Dr. Chris Knippers, who brought with him powerful wisdom. He encouraged us not only to tap our God-given healing abilities, but to see our health challenges, and indeed all of life's challenges, as ways God might be using to direct our lives. Chris skillfully worked with us to help us explore our inner signals. The experience was a breakthrough and became a message that was immediately and profitably used by hundreds of people.

For far too long, we've overlooked the common sense idea of honoring our physical, emotional, and spiritual feedback systems. Intuition has often been dismissed as unpredictable and unreliable. For many God's guidance has been something to yearn for, not something tangible and real. This need not be so.

Common Sense, Intuition, and God's Guidance is a book that vividly brings these ideas to life. In these pages you'll learn how to tap your inner wisdom, integrate your body, mind, and spirit, and empower yourself to experience total well-being on the highest level.

You have been fearfully and wonderfully made, created with powerful capabilities. This book will help you unleash your mighty potential in clear, do-able, and practical steps. I predict that reading this book will be a major turning point in your life.

Common Sense, Intuition, and God's Guidance is an uncommon book filled with ideas that will change your life. Read. Do. Tap your God-given wisdom!

—Greg Anderson
Founder and President,
The Cancer Conquerors Foundation

PREFACE

In this book you will learn what is right—not what is wrong—with you. You will discover you already possess the most valuable resources you need to transform your life.

The principles presented here came out of my personal communication with God and my own growth process as well as the experience of working alongside others in their growth. These principles have so dramatically transformed my life and the lives of others that I felt compelled to share them with the world.

I prayed for just the right words to say; then I prayed for just the right publisher to help me get these important words before the public. I wanted a publisher who would truly understand the message I was trying to convey. From the very beginning of the detailed publishing process, everyone at Thomas Nelson—the editors, the marketing experts, and the publisher—made such concerted effort to fully understand my message that I knew my prayer had been answered.

Practicing the principles written in this book can transform your life and the lives of those around you. Be open as you read and persistent as you live them. I share them with you in love, and wish God's blessing on your life.

CONTENTS

Appendixes

INTRODUCTION

Life is simple, but it's not easy. It's simple in that the principles involved in having a fulfilling existence do not require a great deal of intelligence or talent. Life isn't easy in that we complicate the process so much. We stop listening to truth, and chaos results. We can remind ourselves of the truth, restoring peace and clarity, by heeding the instruction God gives us in common sense, intuition, and His guidance.

We have at our disposal a number of sources of truth. The physical body is a source of feedback that can give us truth about how to function at our best physically. Our physical functioning interacts with our emotions, which also give us feedback about how to function optimally. These sources interact with the mind, which affects all aspects of life. Our bodies and emotions often give us insight that we can call common sense. Through clear mental processes, we can discover truth through intuition. When we pay attention to the feedback of the body, the emotions, and the mind, life is smoother. . . clearer.

The ultimate source of absolute, infallible truth, which is always available to everyone, is God. We often live in chaos because we forget to turn to this source of clear guidance. Having an intimate relationship with God is simple, much more so than with humans, because for every tiny effort we make toward God, He makes major efforts toward us. In fact, God reaches out to us whether we reach out to Him or not. We need only acknowledge and accept God's supreme authority over us in order to experience that intimate relationship.

While God provides clarity, peace, power, and unconditional love, there is another source that brings us confusion, anxiety, weakness, and hostility. It is not within the scope of this book to discuss this negative "source." It is only my desire to acknowledge its existence as a source of some of the chaos in life and the original source of all lies.

As long as we boldly face the realities in our lives and deal with them using all of the sources of truth God has given us, we can live lives with clear minds and healthy bodies and spirits. Chaos will not define our days. Use the feedback that your body gives you; listen to what your emotions tell you about fulfilling your needs. (That means using your common sense.) Allow the mental process of intuition to give you insight into situations and people. And seek a close personal relationship with God, the source of all truth and clarity.

COMMON SENSE, INTUITION, AND GOD'S GUIDANCE

THE COMMON SENSE FEEDBACK OF THE BODY

Y ou are a living miracle. Two microscopic cells joined and began multiplying at a rapid rate, and you were the result. But science can't fully explain the process by which you arrived in this world, nor can any other source.

Equally amazing is the fact that you have survived the multitude of threats to your human existence since that first union of microscopic cells. After birth, dangers you weren't aware of threatened you at every stage of development.

The fact that you are alive right now is a miracle. A force must be protecting and helping you. A reason must exist why this protection and help is keeping you alive and functioning.

Your life has a purpose. God created you to enjoy miraculous processes. To realize your purpose and these miracles you need a keen awareness of the guidance given you by many sources.

At the most basic level, your body is a constant source of guidance we can call common sense. It communicates what you need physically to function at your full potential. It lets you know how to be open and clear to receive communication from even higher sources of guidance and feedback. When you are in great condition physically, you are much more likely to receive clear insights from your mind and emotions concerning what is best for you.

Being physically in tune also brings us closer to experiencing miracles. Jesus Christ was the greatest miracle-worker in history. Healing the body was a specialty of His. When we seek health, in a way we are seeking Christ, because Christ is the healer, the way to health. He is the source of every healing, regardless of how that healing appeared to take place. Healing brings with it a miraculous kind of power that affects every part of our lives. Once the flow of miracles begins in your life, they become a way of life for you. Seeking to be more Christ-like also becomes a natural way of life.

Just the experience of *seeking* health can be an adventure of physical, mental, and spiritual growth. Begin your adventure now by learning the signals of the body and how to interpret them.

Body Signals

The body gives us clear and simple signals when it has needs. Unfortunately, we have an amazing ability to ignore things that are unpleasant or inconvenient for us. The body can give us subtle signals of a need and then block the signal for a time if we don't act on it. After a period of hours or years, depending upon the strength of the need, the body will give us a more aggressive signal. As time passes, the signals become more and more intense until we can no longer ignore them. At this point, the need is urgent, and meeting it will require a lot of pain, expense, and wasted time.

Physical signals often indicate an overworked system. Be aware that one unbalanced system can throw out another system, so pay attention to your entire body to see where your needs lie. Signals may include:

- Low energy
- Digestion and elimination difficulties
- Respiration problems
- Pain (which occurs usually after a need has gone unmet or a system has been over-worked and attacked for too long. You should take even mild pain seriously as a valid physiological warning of overload to your body. Don't mask pain with medication without also seeking to meet the need the pain represents.)
- Skin irritations
- Clouded thinking
- Irritability
- A change in heart rate
- High or low blood pressure
- High or low blood sugar
- Any change in vision, hearing, skin sensitivity, smell, or taste
- Hunger, thirst, and fatigue.

Meeting these simple needs as they arise can keep them from becoming major physical issues.

Dr. O. Carl Simonton, a pioneer in the field of healing the body through the combination of mental and medical processes, says, "Illness is the body's feedback that something is amiss.

Identify changes [in the body] to identify your vulnerabilities. Look at secondary gains to identify your needs."[1]

Simonton says that your body tells you when it needs something. "Secondary gains" are the things we acquire as an illness forces us to get our needs met. For example, a person who believes that it is necessary to work hard, all of the time, to be a good person will develop an illness that forces him to get the rest he has needed all along. Or a woman who believes that it is her duty to take care of and love other people at her own expense will develop an illness that causes her to have other people take care of and love *her*, for a change. Having such an illness forces us to get an essential need met; but this is going about it the *hard* way. Pay attention to your body's signals *before* a serious symptom develops.

You can become very skillful at ignoring the body's signals. You might think you are in perfect health even though a now-forgotten sign once tried to get your attention. You might have paid attention to some signs and ignored others without realizing it. You can get back in touch with your body and its natural communication to you by routinely following some simple steps.

Hearing the Signals

Take time out of your schedule every day to relax for a few minutes and listen to your body's feedback. Most of us become caught up in our daily routines and think we don't have time to get everything done that "needs" to be. It seems almost impossible to find time to do something like sit around and wait for your body to "talk" to you. When serious illness incapacitates you, however, you suddenly have lots of time to lie around. Take a little period of relaxation now, while you are still in control of your time and health.

This relaxation session will not only alert you to any health needs, it will also be a healing activity in itself. Find a quiet place where you can sit or lie down alone for twenty minutes. For some people this means hanging a "Do Not Disturb" sign on the bedroom door or going in the bathroom and lying on blankets and pillows in the bathtub. Others take a drive to a quiet spot and relax in the car. The effort you make to be alone for this short time will be worth it!

In your quiet place, sit or lie down in a comfortable position, close your eyes, and take three deep, slow breaths. Deep breathing naturally relaxes the body. When you are relaxed, the environment can't distract you and you are more open to hearing the natural communication of the body.

In your relaxed state, ask for God's guidance in this process of seeking health through better communication with your body. Through a simple prayer, you are focusing your mind, body, and spirit on the Creator of life and health. With God's guidance you can go only in the right direction.

Achieving deep relaxation of the muscles of your body will heighten your sensitivity to physical feedback. You can attain this by visualizing the muscles of your body loosening up. Picture the muscles of your scalp relaxing, then your forehead, all the muscles of your face, your neck, and your shoulders. (Your neck and shoulder muscles are particularly important, because that is where most people carry the majority of their stress.) Picture the muscles of your hands and arms loosening up and unwinding. See the muscles of your back becoming smoothed and soothed. Imagine your heart muscle and lungs operating efficiently. Envision a relaxed stomach and abdomen. Allow the muscles of your hips, legs, and feet to relax.

Let yourself enjoy that feeling of rest for a few minutes. This exercise will also cause other parts of your body to relax and function more smoothly and efficiently.

Notice if any part of your body does not feel relaxed. If, over the course of several sessions, a particular part of your body feels tense, you might need to pay more attention to the needs of that particular part.

Occasionally a direct insight will come to you about a specific need. For example, you might realize you can treat a strange feeling in your stomach with a simple alteration in your eating habits, or you might become aware of a slight pain you had been ignoring that you could easily treat with more relaxation sessions. See what unique experiences develop for you as you relax. All of your experiences will be pleasant and you will feel safe. You are in God's care, following the plan He intends for you.

Following the plan for your health is an important part of fulfilling the plan for your life. To design anything important we usually use an outline or a blueprint. Your health, one of the most important aspects of your life, needs a blueprint.

You "draw" the blueprint by making a mental picture of the ways you want your body to function. Mental pictures are the means of communication between your mind and body. Your body will "believe" whatever it "sees" in these pictures, and will slowly begin to make the pictures become a reality, because your body adapts itself to what it believes is true. Try creating these mental pictures during your relaxation sessions consistently over a long period of time.

If you want to be thinner, for example, and over a long period of time you picture yourself being thin, you will find you are compelled to do things that will make you thinner. At the same time, your body may begin to process calories more efficiently, giving you a double boost toward fulfilling the mental picture that you have of yourself.

Dr. Simonton discovered that his patients could overcome cancer when they pictured healthy blood cells replacing unhealthy cells. Just think what you could do with less serious health problems. When I first feel the symptoms of a cold coming on, I relax, pray, and picture healthy cells replacing the cold virus. As long as I respond to my body's signal that it needs rest for awhile, the cold goes away. It is important to note that the blueprint works only as you follow common sense health practices and seek competent medical care as needed.

Charles and Rebecca know the value of taking time to attune themselves to body signals and to making a blueprint for health. They are an attractive couple in their late thirties. They have a bright, happy four-year-old daughter and nine-month-old son. Their custom-built, four-bedroom home overlooks a sparkling lake. Until recently, they each owned fine European touring sedans that they drove every day to plush corporate offices where they held full-time, upper-management positions. They were extremely hard workers but managed to find time to be involved in local church leadership as well as to spend quality time with their children.

It all sounded quite wonderful... almost perfect! In fact, at first I wasn't quite sure why they had come to see me. They said they simply weren't as happy as they had expected to be, and both of them thought perhaps they were experiencing a mid-life crisis.

Further investigation revealed that these people had absolutely no relaxation in their lives. They were highly motivated, capable people with big goals and lots of satisfying activities. In fact, the activities had always been so fulfilling that when Charles and Rebecca started feeling unhappy, they just expended their energy a little more, thinking that more activities would bring more happiness. That was one of the reasons they had their second child. When they realized that even this precious baby, whom they adored, had not brought the lasting joy into life they hoped he would, they panicked.

I find it is best to handle any possible physical needs first. (That way, my clients always stay alive long enough to explore any further needs.) In our first session, I completely skipped my usual detailed history-taking and "marriage counseling" (communication skills) and went right into relaxation training. I prescribed daily relaxation sessions for both of them, emphasizing attention to body feedback.

Being the responsible people they are, Charles and Rebecca had daily sessions for even longer than the prescribed minimum twenty minutes. When they returned two weeks later, they were full of news.

Rebecca had rediscovered a slight pain in the back of her head near the base of her skull. She went to her physician immediately, who ran a number of tests. The following day a surgeon removed a small, noncancerous tumor which, he said, could have grown rapidly and blocked some blood flow to her brain. She had already recovered from the minor surgery.

In his relaxation sessions, Charles had noticed an irregular heartbeat. His father, grandfather, and great-grandfather had all experienced serious heart conditions in later life. Charles went to a heart specialist, who put him on a low-fat diet and an exercise program. The doctor assured Charles these would help him avoid the problems the other men in his family had suffered.

Rebecca and Charles were already happier! After a few more months they realized there were other things in their lives they could adjust so they could continue to enjoy good health, prosperity, and their children. They acknowledged that their "good life" might just be slowly killing them. Rebecca and Charles realized that more time for each other and their children would help all of them live longer, happier lives. They also saw they did not really need two luxury cars, a nanny, and a few other things they had come to depend on.

They sold some of them. Charles and Rebecca began sharing one of their jobs at the company, each putting in twenty-five hours a week instead of both of them working fifty hours a week. They shared the domestic responsibilities as well. Everyone had more time to enjoy the *new* good life together.

This beautiful family spared themselves much heartache by listening to the clear messages given them by God. They took time to stop, seek, and listen.

Lifestyles of the Healthy and Happy

As you learn to hear the messages your body sends to you, you can begin to respond by following some simple, common-sense health practices that will affect your whole life. While these practices are simple, they may not be easy, at first, to incorporate into your lifestyle. Any new routine takes a while to feel comfortable. Once these practices *are* in effect, though, you'll wonder how you ever lived without them.

In my personal quest for health and over my twenty-three years in the health care field, I have studied the habits of healthy people. I've found that healthy, happy people generally reflect eight basic characteristics.

1. Healthy people seek high-quality, professional health care.

They find professionals who are willing to work *with* them rather than *on* them. They stay aware enough of their own bodies to know whether or not a treatment is working and they are not afraid to tell their physicians if they disagree with their treatment. They follow conventional medical wisdom but are open to alternative treatments. Some people go to a physician as well as a professional from one or more other health professions, such as a dietician, chiropractor, psychotherapist, or a massage therapist. The important thing is healthy people know when to seek help and they find it, no matter how hard they have to try.

Medical care is often the vehicle for miracles. When I was eleven years old, I was in a landslide in a Southern California canyon. My skull and brain were crushed so badly the first doctors I was taken to said there was nothing they could do for me. At a hospital in the next town, a neurosurgeon pieced together as much of my skull as he could, but he saw no hope that I would recover from the brain damage. He predicted that I would live in a vegetative state for as little as a few hours or as long as few months, but inevitably I would die. My parents insisted the medical team do everything it could while they did everything they could.

The medical team called in specialists; my family prayed, along with friends of theirs all over the world. The prognosis remained grim, but my parents' spiritual outlook was joyful. My parents *were* joyful, even before miraculously, three days later, I opened my eyes and recognized them. I had complete brain and body functioning restored within a month! I took an ocean cruise, then returned to my classes in a program for gifted children, starred in a musical, and completed my classes with A's. God used a medical team in conjunction with loving, prayerful people to restore a battered brain to normal functioning.

2. Healthy people prioritize rest and relaxation.

No matter what the problem, rest always helps. Healthy people take regular periods of time to relax, giving healthy cells a chance to regenerate and healthy attitudes and perspectives a chance to develop. This is one of the most simple and most often overlooked means of gaining clarity of mind, body, and spirit.

A body at rest can do its routine maintenance and repair work. The mind also gets a break from dealing with all the stimulation we subject it to. It can begin to regroup its functions and influence without a lot of interruptions. Thinking pleasant thoughts and daydreaming can actually be constructive, especially for someone who deals with serious or complicated issues. We've all had the experience of working very hard to think of a solution to a problem, giving up in desperation, then coming back to the problem after a period of rest and seeing the solution clearly. Math and the sciences recognize this a-ha! phenomenon. You can cure "writer's block" this same way. Giving the mind periods of rest is essential.

Relaxation periods are one of the most nurturing things you can do for yourself. You'll find it very satisfying to give yourself the message that you deserve a break. The ultimate source of nurturing, God, can become more clear to you during times of rest. When you are not listening to all the other voices in your life that tell you what to do, where to go, and who you should be, you have the opportunity to turn to God and hear from the true Authority on life.

3. Healthy people are productive.

Healthy people look forward to going to work, because it gives them the sense they are doing something useful. They also enjoy leaving work at the end of the day, because whatever they do after work also has purpose and fulfillment.

You can be productive in your activities by doing what you have desire and passion to do, by trying new activities from time to time, and by accepting challenges. There are opportunities everywhere you turn. For example, no one has yet stamped out the epidemic of loneliness. You would find being part of the solution extremely fulfilling. Pollution is another desperate problem. You can find many ways to contribute to the effort to clean up our environment.

You have what it takes to make a big difference in many areas of life. Look around you and observe your family, work associates, friends, church, community. See what you can do to make all of your current activities meaningful to others as well as to you.

4. Healthy people eat nutritiously.

It's not difficult to do, either. Despite what radical food faddists say, nutritious food is available almost anywhere you go. We know so much more about nutrition now than ever before. We've learned that most adults need only three to six ounces of a complete protein source daily; less than 30 percent of daily calorie intake from fat; and a generous amount of fresh vegetables, fruit, and whole-grain carbohydrates. People on this kind of diet feel better and avoid physical problems. I've also noticed that healthy, happy people are not obsessive or compulsive about their healthy diets. They occasionally have their favorite desserts! It's okay because . . .

5. Healthy people exercise.

This opens a flow of physical, mental, and spiritual processes. As blood circulates through the body, it stimulates other healthy physical processes, which in turn clear mental functioning, enabling us to open our minds to God. Exercise is another way of giving yourself a "tune-up." Physical fitness experts recommend some continuous movement which stimulates the heart (such as walking, swimming, dancing, bicycling, upper-body calisthenics) at least four times a week for twenty minutes. Newer research indicates that shorter but more frequent periods of exercise are just as effective, for example, ten minutes, three times a day. Often exercise is a stimulant when you feel fatigued.

6. Healthy people have supportive relationships.

A person who is unconditionally supportive of you can help you live a longer, more fulfilling life. Researchers at Stanford University discovered that patients who had life-threatening illnesses and attended a support group lived longer than patients who didn't. Support groups have also benefited patients with less-threatening illnesses. People in these support groups accept and respect each other regardless of their social/ political views, regardless of mistakes they have made, and regardless of their emotional or physical conditions. Support groups offer people places to be themselves. These types of relationships offer people reasons to live.

So often people don't put all the effort they could into staying alive because what they have to live for is so stressful and meaningless. Even *one* supportive relationship can allow a person to be who she or he is without pretense and bring the joy of meaningful interaction. A healing, spiritual quality exists in this type of relationship because in order to give and receive this unconditional support, you must have the presence of God in the relationship.

7. *Healthy people laugh and play.*

You might think that healthy people laugh and play because they are happy, but often the opposite is true. Scientific research has shown that the body produces healthy blood cells when you laugh. Consequently, laughter enhances the immune system and for some people it also reduces pain. I know a woman who had foot surgery without anesthesia but felt little or no pain because she laughed the entire time. She didn't even have pain in the recovery room afterward.

You don't need a stimulus for laughter. Your body will still produce healthy chemicals even if it doesn't know why you are laughing. (It *never* knows why you are laughing anyway.)

Learn to see the humor in everyday situations. Learn to laugh at yourself. In order for something to be truly funny, *you* are the only one who really needs to find it humorous. Other people joining in on the fun just multiplies the effects of the laughter.

That is one reason why play is so important. It provides a lot of material for humor and laughter. Play can be any activity that has noncompetitive fun as its only purpose.

You can play alone. In fact, I recommend a certain amount of playtime alone. The whole concept of an adult *playing* might sound very immature, but that is exactly why you need to do it. Being an adult creates a lot of pressure on you. Let yourself lighten up and loosen up!

Schedule play times. Start simply. Think back to when you were a child (the younger, the better) and what you enjoyed then. Observe children playing and adapt their activities to your adult lifestyle. Ask other adults what they do for noncompetitive play. Playfaire, Inc. is an organization in Berkeley, California, that teaches adults to play. Its founder and "emperor" (as he likes to be called), Dr. Matt Weinstein, has a number of books with play activities for adults (now, don't get the wrong idea!).

Learn to play, and most of all, laugh often. New dimensions of life will open up to you and things will seem a whole lot clearer.

8. Healthy people have faith.

The belief that there is a power greater than themselves affects everything that well-adjusted people do. Belief in God gives them a sense of security. God is experienced as being loving, forgiving, and powerful; therefore, healthy people can trust their entire futures to His love and power.

Healthy, happy people face their own shortcomings bravely because they know God not only forgives them but helps them overcome their faults. They trustingly surrender their entire lives to God. (Usually this surrender is a lengthy process and for some it can take a lifetime. The important thing is that you maintain faith throughout the process.) God is the ultimate authority in the lives of well-adjusted people. Developing faith will give you the peace, security, and clarity you seek.

By adopting these eight characteristics you can meet nearly all of your body's needs, bringing health to your physical functioning. Hearing your body's signals is following one of the forms of guidance God gives us.

Be patient with yourself and persistent with your efforts. We all learn and grow at different paces. Where your health and happiness levels happen to be at this moment has nothing to do with your own personal worth. You are still a miracle, regardless of your attainments or even your efforts to attain. What *is* important is that you persist in your quest for health, happiness, and clarity.

THE COMMON SENSE FEEDBACK OF THE EMOTIONS

She was twenty-two and beautiful, with long, chestnut hair, clear brown eyes, and silky skin free of any makeup that would hide her natural vitality. She was wearing a simple cotton dress with a high collar and long sleeves as she sat down in my office that afternoon. I suspected she was of a conservative religious background and was in the office of a Christian counselor seeking some comfort from her shocking new life in Southern California.

Frequent unassuming smiles and her articulate speech revealed a quiet, charming personality. She was a vision of innocence. That is why, when she began to tell her story, I thought someone was playing an elaborate joke on me.

Mindy had grown up in a conservative, affluent Orange County family. Her mother, father, and younger sister all enjoyed excellent health, high intelligence, impeccable reputations, and close, loving relationships. It all came to an abrupt and mind-spinning end when her father died suddenly while driving her home from her first day as a high school senior.

All the love, security, and privilege she had known came to a tragic halt. Despite the wealth her father had accumulated, Mindy, her mother, and her sister found themselves in financial stress when unscrupulous business partners finagled away the family's fortune. The women had to go to work to try to keep their home, their last semblance of security.

Mindy's mother and sister seemed to recover from the shock of the father's death within a year, but Mindy's grief grew into anger and, finally, intense rebellion.

Mindy had a girlfriend at school who always dressed in the latest fashions and drove a nice car, even though she was from a poor family. Mindy wanted to know Shawna's secret, so Shawna introduced her to Randolf, her wealthy "boyfriend." He had a lucrative business in which Shawna was employed. All she had to do was go on "dates" with wealthy businessmen, and take home two to four hundred dollars an hour, depending on how the date ended.

Mindy was appalled. She immediately cut off her association with Shawna and tried to renew her relationships with her mother and sister. But the financial problems at home were mounting, and no one had any time to spend with Mindy. Besides, the consuming materialism of Orange County was making Mindy feel embarrassed to go anywhere without wearing stylish clothes and driving a nice car. She felt completely insecure as it was. She had to do *something* to help herself and her family overcome their compounding sense of loss. She thought if only she could make a lot of money, she and her family would be happy again.

Mindy called Shawna. As much as it terrified and disgusted her, Mindy asked to talk to Randolf about working for him just long enough to pull her family out of financial distress. Randolf was delighted. The handsome, seemingly sophisticated man even promised to be Mindy's boyfriend, which she found strangely comforting. She felt an acceptance and belonging she had missed over the last year.

Five years later, Mindy was sitting before me an employee of the infamous, now-defunct Mustang Ranch, a legalized brothel in Nevada. She had paid impeccable attention to her health, noticing every signal from her body that might indicate a medical need. Terrified of the diseases women in that line of work get, she had thorough medical checkups twice monthly. She was, mercifully, in good physical health.

However, something vital was completely missing from her profile of overall health, and that was what brought her to me: She had no trace of genuine emotion. She had the looks, voice inflection, and appropriate phrases and gestures, but she was completely void of real feeling. She had learned to act out a role, one that appealed to high-paying customers.

The problem began when her cries for help in the days following her father's death went unheeded. The signs had been there for teachers, relatives, friends, and church staff to see: her unmasked grief, scathing anger, blatant rebellion. But everyone assumed this was a phase and would pass. When it didn't, they decided she was just a nasty person who should be "taught a lesson." She complicated her problem by trying to help her family in a job that required her to wipe out her sensitive, vulnerable, little girl emotions in order to be able to function at all.

Mindy had once been an innocent, happy young person. She had grown into a responsible, straight-A student. She was a virgin when she first went to see Randolf. She suffered unbearable emotional torment when she lost her virginity and during every job assignment during the following months as well. Eventually Mindy discovered the human ability to block out emotional pain and, eventually, all feeling.

We all possess the capacity to block out our emotions, but it usually happens to most of us subtly, not dramatically as with Mindy. Emotions are a phenomenal source of invaluable, life-giving feedback. Every emotion has a valuable purpose in our lives. Unfortunately, our society teaches us that some emotions are "good" and some are "bad." Emotions are neither. They don't fall into the category of things that can be "judged." Emotions just are. We can act on them in good or bad ways, but we should experience all emotions to the fullest. It's important to learn adaptive means for dealing with them, for your emotions give you priceless information about how to make your life more fulfilling! Listen to them and learn from them to avoid becoming emotionally dead.

Because Mindy had dulled her emotions, she could no longer receive feedback from them to tell her how to meet her needs and recover from all she had been through. Not surprisingly anger, guilt, sadness, and fear seem to be the most difficult emotions to process effectively. They're also the emotions we often discourage each other from expressing. As we see in the example of Mindy's experience, when repressed, negative emotions lodge deep in your mind and begin to subtly effect everything you think, say, and do. Because you've stopped actively feeling angry or guilty or sad, you may think these emotions are gone. However they're still in your subconscious and you do express them, although indirectly. They don't go away just because you ignore them.

Emotions expressed indirectly usually have a negative effect on everyone who sends or receives them because they prevent everyone's needs being met. Repressed emotions can also make you seriously ill, both physically and emotionally. Unexpressed anger can be especially dangerous, because it can develop into a sense of hopelessness. Such despair is often found in people who eventually develop life-threatening illnesses. When you express emotions openly and with regard for the feelings of others, they become a means of building closer relationships, of improving health, and of getting everyone's needs met.

Emotions give us clues for how to get our needs and those of others met most effectively. They are a means to clear thinking and productive functioning in life. We operate optimally when our psychological as well as physical needs are met.

The Nine Psychological/Emotional Needs

I have adapted nine psychological/emotional needs from the eight needs identified by psychology researcher and consultant Dr. Taibi Kahler. This research has been used in the NASA space program.[1]

I. The Need for Recognition of Work

Recognition for the things we do gives us incentive to continue growing and being productive. We will repeat whatever behavior gets attention and will try new behaviors to see if those also get attention. This is a law of human nature. If our undesirable behavior receives more attention—even negative—than desirable behavior, we will repeat it. Consistently ignored behavior will eventually cease.

If you are not receiving the attention you deserve and need, you might be feeling guilty, depressed, and/or angry. You might need to seek more attention for your accomplishments by applying the assertiveness skills explained later in this chapter.

2. The Need for Recognition for Conviction

Receiving attention for your values and beliefs affirms your importance. You have developed your values and beliefs according to your unique experiences in life as your individual feelings and thought mechanisms processed them. No one has experienced life exactly the way you have. Even if people disagree with your views, they need to recognize your perspective as being valid for you, withholding their judgment or criticism. You also need to be open to hearing other people's views. That is how you change and grow and expand your perspectives. Your views will, hopefully, change and grow as you do. You don't need this affirmation from everyone, but only from a few people who are close to you.

Adults do much damage to children and adolescents by dismissing their views as being immature and silly. Young people need to receive recognition for their current beliefs so that they will feel encouraged to continue to explore their values. When they receive respect, they give respect and will be more open to hearing varied points of view (including those of adults).

If you feel insignificant, depressed, or angry, perhaps your values and beliefs are not being respected. Again, an assertive approach will eventually bring you the recognition you deserve.

3. The Need for Contact

The type and degree of human contact an individual needs depends on the individual and what is happening in his or her life. Certain temperament types want a great deal of close interaction. Others want primarily to be "observers" of the lives of others without too much involvement. Whatever the degree of need, to have meaning in their lives everyone needs the presence of other people, and everyone needs at least one *close* relationship. A close or intimate relationship is one in which two people trust and respect one another. In such a relationship both people openly express their feelings and opinions, values and affection, knowing the other person will listen, care, and accept whatever is being expressed.

All of these aspects of close relationships have a healing, sustaining effect. People who have at least one close friend live longer and happier lives. Doctors have found the stimulation and unconditional acceptance that even animals bring to the lives of the physically and mentally ill have a sustaining effect.

People with a high need for contact want playful, fun interaction with the other people in their lives, which can help develop their senses of humor. Humor brings balance and perspective to life.

You can meet your own need for contact, whether it's high or low, by trying to find the playful, child-like side of yourself and by seeing the humor in situations and people you might usually take seriously. You can do this by asking yourself how a playful child would respond to that person or circumstance, how humor might fit the situation.

Some signs that you might need more inter-action include feelings of emptiness (lack of feel-ing), sadness, or insecurity. Just going out in public sometimes helps temporarily. Participat-ing in church, civic, political, and interest groups often offers good opportunities to develop relationships. A great opportunity exists in support groups, for these groups gather positive people who help one another overcome common problems with support and acceptance. Psychologists and counselors can refer you to a group that would be appropriate for you. Whatever you do, get involved with positive, open, supportive people who recognize you for the miracle you are! (For suggestions on finding such people, see Appendix A.)

4. The Need to Be Recognized as a Person

Beyond mere interaction, we all need unconditional love. This develops in a relationship after you have made some mistakes and your friend still accepts you, supports you, and helps you feel good about yourself. Unconditional love says, "Regardless of what you have or have not accomplished, regardless of what we do or do not have in common, I regard you as important and valuable to me, and I am going to cherish our relationship."

This kind of love is the most healing kind. It makes life richer and more valuable than anything else in the world. Be patient in seeking and developing it. When trouble arises in a relationship and people stop being open with each other, love fades. You must remain open and take the risk of being hurt to develop unconditional love.

If you feel like you are just surviving rather than thriving, you likely need to seek unconditional love in your life. Look for relationships with people who are attentive to you in small ways, such as paying attention to you when you talk. Such people are usually the ones who can help meet your deeper needs as well. Also become aware of some of the more subtle ways people show they care about you. You might already be receiving a lot more love than you realize.

5. The Need for Time Structure

Unless we have boundaries around our time schedules, other people can control us. Then we would never have any time to do the things we want to do, to get our own needs met, or to do anything creative.

You may feel that way right now. You may have been so concerned about not being "selfish" that you've exploited yourself, which is very harmful.

You need to learn what your individual needs are for time control so you can set boundaries. This is essentially just fixing a schedule for yourself and sticking to it. It does not have to be inflexible, but you need to know you are the one who controls your time.

We have varying degrees of need for controlling our time. Some people actually feel more secure having someone tell them what to do. Others want almost full control of their own schedules. When you have not set and maintained time boundaries, you might feel pressured, scattered, unproductive, uncreative, fatigued, insecure, or confused. Be assertive enough to set your own limits.

6. The Need for Solitude

Part of the reason we need control of our time is to help us get other needs met. A need very closely related to that of time boundaries is the need for solitary reflection. Reflecting is a time to pray for guidance and then allow your thoughts to wander. When we do this, we often intuitively realize solutions to problems, discover needs that are not being met, see ways we can help other people solve problems, discern how to improve our communication with God, and many other insights.

A lack of solitary reflection can result in many feelings, such as confusion, depression, irritability, and fatigue. We all need a certain amount of solitude each day; but again, how much time depends on the individual. This is recharging time, when we refill our batteries physically, emotionally, mentally, and spiritually. You might need a great deal more or much less recharging time than those you live with. Honor your own needs.

Solitary time is one of the most neglected areas of personal health care in many people I counsel. The people with the most pressing demands are the ones who need solitary reflection the most. It improves your efficiency to a greater degree than anything else, so that a small amount of time spent in solitude equals a large amount of time in terms of greater productivity later.

7. The Need for Sensory Stimulation

Stimulation of the senses is a need that, for the most part, is met by everyday life. We all like a certain degree of variety in sights, sounds, textures, smells, and tastes. Become aware of your own level of need for stimulation of the five senses and choose activities to meet it. For example, a person needing lots of sensory stimulation who works in a routine, highly structured job might feel overwhelmingly bored. Allow yourself all of the variety you need, without becoming over-stimulated.

8. The Need for Incidence

Incidence means a need for action and excitement in life. A person with a high need for incidence will be a risk-taker with a high energy level. He or she will *make* excitement happen.

The need for incidence might be related to the universal need in human beings for a sense of purpose. That is essentially what gives a person a reason to live. Most everyone has faced a moment in which he or she has asked, "Is life worth all of this struggle?"

Many people experience enough significant losses in their lives, sometimes all at once, that they feel they have no reason to live. Bankruptcy, death of a spouse, divorce, incurable disease, and loss of career are just a few experiences that cause people to question the meaning of their existences. Whether we experience significant losses or not, we all need a reason to get out of bed every day and to keep striving to accomplish something. The philosopher Nietzsche said, "He who has a *why* to live can bear with almost any *how*." [2]

Dr. Victor Frankl is the great Viennese psy-

chiatrist who revolutionized the field of psychia-
try with his perspectives after losing everything
in a Nazi concentration camp. He lost his family,
friends, career, money, some of his health, and
even his human dignity. Because of this personal
holocaust, he began to question what keeps people struggling to live through another day, even
when facing constant terror. Through his ques-
tioning, he realized the driving force in the lives
of survivors was their personal search for meaning
in their lives. They kept going just to find some
sort of purpose in what they were going through.

After his release, Dr. Frankl wrote *Man's
Search for Meaning* and began a new form of
therapy called logotherapy. "According to logotherapy, we can discover this meaning in life in
three different ways: (1) by creating a work or
doing a deed; (2) by experiencing something or
encountering someone; and (3) by the attitude we
take toward unavoidable suffering." [3]

You can find meaning in your life through
your job, volunteer work, recreational activities,
and the relationships in which you give and
receive unconditional love. Search for the activities
and relationships that give you a sense of purpose. These will not necessarily be ones that are

easy for you; we often find meaning in activities and relationships that are a challenge.

Meaning can also come out of the losses and problems we encounter in life. I would never have experienced the indescribable joy and peace I know now had I not reached a point in my life when I decided I had been through all the suffering I could possibly bear, and my only option was to find happiness. After losing everything of meaning in my life, I found greater meaning than I had ever before known. Something about suffering can cause us to take a more enlightened view of life. Suffering can open you to ideas and options you would never have considered otherwise. The important thing to do when suffering is to keep searching! You *will* find meaning in your life.

9. The Need for a Relationship With God

I believe this is also an essential need in humans because it is necessary for fulfillment of an individual's sense of identity. We can each know who we really are as we know the One who created us. God is the only Authority who can truly know and communicate why we're here. If you are feeling a sense of alienation, lack of fulfillment, sadness, loss, or emptiness, you might need to seek a close, personal relationship with God.

When we make sure all of our psychological/emotional needs are met, we can then receive important feedback from our emotions that will serve to guide us. Before we talk about this, we need to see how having unmet needs creates unhealthy patterns that block this guidance.

Unmet Needs

When any of your needs go unmet for too long, negative patterns of relating to people and situations evolve. One pattern that can develop is blaming people and circumstances for your unhappiness. You might believe someone or something has control of your life; therefore, it is someone else's fault you are unhappy. The truth is you have a lot more control of your life than sometimes appears. Find that control, and take it.

People who develop an attitude of blame and find their needs are still not met begin to experience resentment and rage. These people go from merely blaming others to being angry much of the time. They lose their tempers too often and seem to have chips on their shoulders. Controlling other people becomes their goal. There is hope for them when they realize they do have control of their own lives.

Self-abasement is another result of unmet needs. People who do this are close to abandoning the quest to get their needs met. They feel unworthy. Unless some ray of hope comes into their lives, these people begin to withdraw from others and even from God. At this point, they can be saved from despair by something as simple as a smile from a stranger. Some people who have been on the brink of suicide report deciding to live when someone simply smiled and said, "Hello." Sometimes that is just enough encouragement to restore a person's hope for that day.

Hopelessness is the ultimate result of not getting one's needs met. People in despair often don't take advantage of help that is offered to them. They don't even recognize when a need is finally met, because they have ceased to even look for such things. Getting to this point in need-deprivation is dangerous. It is very close to emotional death. Whatever happens in your life, you must hold onto hope. Those who have hope do find help.

Assertiveness and Your Human Rights

In order to get your needs met and to get along with people, you must be assertive. Many people expect those closest to them to know what their needs are and how to meet them without being told. These unassertive people won't inconvenience anyone by asking for help. However, unassertive people think they should meet other people's needs any time they are asked to. At the other extreme are people who demand that all of their needs be met at their convenience, and in their way. These overly aggressive types might get some of their needs met, but it is always at the expense of others.

Assertive people ask for what they want and need and can define the limits of what they are willing to do for others. In order to be assertive, you must first develop an attitude of respect for yourself and others. When you respect yourself, you naturally seek fulfillment of your needs. You also naturally know what you are or are not willing to do for others and set those limits when necessary. Having respect allows you to do all of this in a way that preserves and enhances other people's self-esteem.

You have certain rights as a human being that

you might not be aware of and which you might not be protecting.

- You have the right to have any emotion at any time. Emotions are natural and beneficial. What we do with them is another matter. Feel free to feel. No one has the right to criticize the emotions you have.
- You have the right to express your feelings when doing so will not be harmful to another person.
- You have the right to be heard.
- You have the right to ask for help in getting any of your needs met.
- You have the right to decline to help another person when you believe it would be best to do so and he or she will not be harmed. (Remember, others also have the right to decline your requests.)
- You have the right to your own opinions.
- You have the right to express your opinions in the interest of meeting a legitimate need when doing so will not harm another person.

Notice that all of these rights require careful attention to the rights and feelings of others.

They are meant only to help you get your needs met, which will pave the way to clear emotional feedback.

Keep in Touch

We are all being urged these days to get in touch with our feelings. If you are not sure how to do this or are not even sure what that means, you might want to try this exercise.

Take at least twenty minutes alone in a quiet place to relax, close your eyes, take a few deep, slow breaths, and ask God to reveal to you any emotions you need to be aware of. Your thoughts might wander, but stay in that relaxed state, asking for God's guidance. You might repeat this exercise once a day for several days, until you feel you are more aware of your true emotional state. When you begin to know what you are feeling, write down these feelings. Then look at the list of psychological/emotional needs to see which ones are being met and which are not.

Make a specific plan for getting your needs met. Start by talking to a supportive person about your feelings and needs. Get feedback about how you might most effectively respond to your own emotions and needs. Support can come from friends, relatives, pastors, priests, professional counselors, or psychotherapists. The important thing is that the person you talk to meets the criteria of a "supportive person," and that you are open with him or her. (See Appendix A.)

Staying in touch with your feelings requires effort, but it is essential for receiving clear, common sense communication on what you really need to live the abundant life that you, a miracle, were meant to live.

THE
COMMON SENSE
FEEDBACK
OF THE MIND

"I just need to clear my head" is a common plea. Unfortunately our minds easily become cluttered and are often more so than we realize. All the stresses, both large and small, that we experience during the course of a day, as well as all the events we observe, are processed through our minds. Everything we do, everything we anticipate doing, and many of the things we have done in the past are all on our minds. Whether the thoughts are pleasant or stressful, they will have an influence on our ability to handle new information. Our minds are capable of handling more data than any computer now in existence; but too much information coming in at once can cause a temporary overload.

This is when your mind can shut down. This shutdown can be partial or complete and can last for varying lengths of time. We all have experienced brief lapses of memory, such as forgetting someone's name. Someone might tell us something, looking us right in the eye, yet we don't hear a word of it. Usually it isn't the aging process that causes us to be forgetful or "spaced out." It's cluttered thinking.

It is extremely important to have a clear mind since it has a profound influence on every aspect of your functioning: physical, emotional, psychological, mental, and spiritual. The influence of the mind is so tremendous and pervasive that many people believe it has "power" and build religions around it. True power, in the life of a human, can come only from God. We can tap into God's power on a spiritual level, but in the human sense the mind has *influence*, not power. Even so, phenomenal things can be accomplished by directing and harnessing the mind's influence. When God directs this part of us, incredible things can be accomplished.

Levels of Thought

We are aware of only a small portion of our thought processes. The mind has different levels of thought. The one we are always cognizant of is the conscious level. Conscious thoughts are the ones we control. We decide where to go, what to do, whom to see, and how to do what we want to do. With our conscious minds we form the words we want to say and decide what we want to listen to. We use our conscious minds to make plans, decisions, evaluations, interpretations, and judgments. But, as we know, plans don't always turn out the way we want, the decisions we make are not always the best ones, and there are many ways to evaluate, interpret, and judge a particular situation or person.

Our unconscious minds influence the plans we make, which decisions we choose, and the ways we perceive situations. They contain more information than we can store in our conscious minds. It would be unwieldy for us to have all the information we have accumulated over a lifetime constantly in front of us.

The unconscious contains both memories that are easily accessible and others that can be tapped only with a great deal of effort. It contains

very poignant memories of strong emotional/
psychological needs that were never fully met.
The conscious mind can forget extremely trau-
matic events, yet store them in vivid detail in the
unconscious.

For example, I have no recollection of being
in a landslide, even though those present say I
was fully alert. I yelled and even pushed my
friend out of the path of the boulder before it
struck me. Witnesses say I was conscious for a
while afterward and I screamed for help. Fortu-
nately, I am unable to recall any of this even after
being told the details of the incident. Yet my
unconscious mind is holding that information.

The mind is often compared to an iceberg.
Only the smallest portion of an iceberg is visible
above the surface of the water, just as the conscious mind reveals only the surface of all our
thought information. The largest portion of the
iceberg is hidden below the surface, just as the
unconscious portion of the mind is below the surface of thought, and its contents are not obvious.
These below-surface thoughts significantly affect
you. Even though you might think you have
completely forgotten an incident that made you
extremely angry, you could still be making decisions and having perceptions based on the anger,

which is still stored in your unconscious mind. If you had expressed your anger in some constructive way (confronted the person who offended you, for example), likely you would not have been negatively influenced by the past incident. A stored emotion does have an energy that influences us either positively or negatively, depending on how the emotion was dealt with at the time the incident occurred.

Unconscious Beliefs

These stored emotions form thoughts which become beliefs. Our beliefs, both conscious and unconscious, strongly influence the outcome of our lives. A person who believes she is an attractive, bright, good person is going to put herself in situations that are to her advantage. On the other hand, a person who thinks of himself as unattractive, slow, and ordinary is going to put himself in situations and with people who confirm his ideas about himself.

Most people want to be happy and successful, yet relatively few people are, even though they think they are trying to accomplish those goals. The unconscious belief system sometimes overrides the conscious goals of a person. An unconscious belief that you are unworthy or incapable of happiness and success can make you unconsciously do things that sabotage your efforts to be happy and successful. Because the belief is unconscious, you wouldn't notice this happening and would be puzzled why you couldn't seem to reach your goals. The reverse is also true. Some people consciously think of themselves as ordinary, yet their unconscious belief systems drive them to be successful. There are many accomplished people who can't explain their good fortune; they think they're "just lucky." Indeed, they were lucky to have someone in their lives who programmed them with positive beliefs about themselves and about life.

The messages parents, teachers, ministers, and other people of influence give a child have a profound effect on his or her belief system. Experts believe what you hear and believe in your first six years will affect you all the rest of your life. Parents do serious harm by calling their children "bad," thinking the children will be motivated to not do something that earns them that label. But actually the child's unconscious stores the label as part of his or her sense of self-esteem, and inevitably the child will be compelled to act it out.

The Chain of Influence

By changing your thoughts and beliefs, you can change your behaviors and feelings. The usual chain of influence begins with a thought. The thought develops into a belief about your self or life in general. The belief produces emotions. The emotions result in actions or behaviors, which are attempts to fulfill a need represented by the emotions. Behaviors also can be attempts to escape unpleasant emotions.

If I have been treated with love and respect, I am going to think I am a lovable, respectable guy. That thought will develop into the belief that I deserve good things in life. That belief is going to cause me to feel confident and to act in lovable, respectable ways, which will help me to seek people and opportunities consistent with my beliefs, feelings, and behavior. (I will not listen to people who put me down, for example, because I will immediately recognize they are wrong.) In seeking people and opportunities that fit my beliefs, I will meet other loving, respectable people—the types who succeed. By joining forces, we will do things that improve our lives and the lives of others.

Micky Stephens is an octogenarian who

knows the influence of beliefs on a person's life. Micky lived a fairly normal life. She did all that was expected of an attractive young woman of her day. She married, had children, and took care of their home life. During her early life, she did not do anything particularly noteworthy.

When she was thirty-five, however, everything went topsy-turvy. She developed a very rare disease, Guillain-Barré syndrome, an illness similar to polio; it causes paralysis and particularly affects the respiratory system.

A year later, Micky developed multiple sclerosis. Some days she was unable to walk. She rarely had much energy. However, she immediately told herself she was not going to suffer, be depressed, or quit being active. Even on days when she felt bad, she got out of bed and out of the house to help someone who had a need and to be involved in her children's lives.

Micky felt a determination build inside herself. She was beating these insidious diseases by developing a belief system that said she could!

At age forty-two she developed another rare disease: Wolf-White Parkinsons. This condition is a defect in the electrical impulses of the heart that can cause debilitating irregular heartbeats. Wouldn't it be natural for anyone in Micky's situation to believe there was nothing to be gained from her life? Not Micky. She refused to believe her situation was hopeless. She went to nursing school and missed only two days of the whole program. She graduated with honors, despite having grown up in a family that told her she was "the cute child, not the smart one." Micky's illnesses had given her a determination that helped her to overcome not only her immediate situations, but also her childhood programming. She went on to work in a leper colony on Kauai, and helped hundreds of hopeless, rejected people find meaning in their lives.

A few years ago, when she was in her late seventies, Micky developed an incurable form of cancer that spread through her body. She still would not give up, even though the prognosis was that she had just two to six months to live. She asked God to heal her, repeated the Twenty-third Psalm and the words "God is healing me" throughout the day, wore a pin that said "I expect a miracle," and thought of the people she could help by staying alive.

Today no trace of cancer exists in her body. Her physicians call her "the miracle lady." She works in a major hospital, is on the board of directors of her church, does hospice counseling, helps lead two support groups for cancer patients and a Bible study, aids handicapped individuals with their daily activities, and is the life of many a party with her wildly funny jokes.

Micky's belief system has enabled her to overcome an ordinary childhood and a physically devastating adulthood to become a bright, happy, fulfilled woman of profound influence and healing.

You can have a belief system that will enable you to do anything you want to do with your life. You might have had extreme physical and emotional trauma throughout your life. You might have inflicted trauma on others. You might see no way out of your problems. But you can overcome whatever situations existed in your past, whatever situations exist in the present, and whatever appears will happen in your future. All you need to be the person you want to be is a relationship with someone who believes in you and a belief system consistent with the truth about you. You are a miracle.

(For more information about how to improve your belief system, see Appendix B.)

Ultimate Clarity of Mind

Once you've squared away your belief system, you will achieve even greater clarity of mind by freeing yourself from worry. Worry is the foremost deterrent to clear thinking. You usually learn it from a significant person, or people, in your life. Worry clouds your thinking so that it becomes more and more difficult to find solutions to problems. A calm, rational approach to problems is always much more effective.

Breaking the worry habit is usually accomplished gradually. You can begin by disciplining yourself, one hour at a time, to replace worry thoughts with calm, confident, reassuring thoughts and faith. By telling yourself you have to focus your thoughts in a more positive direction for only one hour, you won't be so overwhelmed with trying to stop all at once. You can begin by having one worry-free hour a day, progress to two hours a day for a few days, and so on. Soon you will be having entire days that are worry-free.

You will probably have to work on this one for a very long time. Be persistent and very patient with yourself. Some people develop specific thoughts ahead of time to replace worry thoughts. Some people rehearse new beliefs, say a brief prayer, quote a Scripture passage, or think of a key word (such as "calm," "peace," "joy") when they catch themselves worrying. The important thing is to keep fighting!

A worry-free mind is a clear, healthy mind open to all the possibilities and blessings God has for your life. You will experience life more fully as you develop more realistic beliefs and as you free your mind of the clutter of worry. Clear your mind so you can be open to receive all the guidance and blessings that are yours.

THE
INSIGHT OF
INTUITION

Have you ever had the experience of feeling slightly uncomfortable with a person or in a situation for no obvious reason? You might have experienced an unexplainable urge to go to a certain location, talk to a certain person, or make a certain choice, even when these urges did not seem logical. Maybe you followed the urges and got positive results. Maybe you ignored them and later discovered you were disappointed with the ultimate outcome of a situation.

We are all equipped with a form of guidance that was designed to keep us out of trouble and help us make wise choices, even when we do not have all of the information we want to make them. You can accurately judge which situations and relationships are appropriate for you, where you need to be, and what you need to do without having all of the facts you think you need.

The ability to *know* the nature of a situation, person, or thing without prior experience comes from the innate gift of intuition. Intuition does not use conscious logic or reason. Most of the thought processes involved take place at the unconscious level of your mind.

Our conscious minds are aware of the world around us. We use our conscious minds most of the time. Our minds take information from people, situations, and things in the environment and combine it with memory and experience to help us make decisions and to help us function.

The unconscious mind, however, is the largest portion of our minds. It stores vast amounts of information, much of which we are totally unaware. These information-gatherers were given to us when we were created to help us function more smoothly and effectively. It is much like having an on-board super-computer. Whether you know it or not, you do have this "equipment"! And you use it frequently. Your conscious mind relies on your subconscious for information. Some people might think their "super-computers" are defective or missing because most of us do not use those parts of our minds enough to be aware of them. Learning to listen to your intuition is one of the best ways to get to know this part of yourself.

Intuition relies on the information stored in the unconscious from memories and past experiences, new data from our current environment, and information that our bodies and emotions give to the unconscious. Intuition takes information from the immediate situation or person that we need to evaluate and combines it with all of the facts and teachings stored in the unconscious to create a definite impression or decision.

We often ignore this valuable, sometimes vital, source of guidance because many of us have the tendency to give credibility only to what we can prove with our conscious thoughts and the facts we can observe. We hesitate to act on our hunches. Certainly some things require observable proof before we can believe they are valid; we can't afford to make all our decisions based only on impressions or emotions.

But intuition is not a hunch, nor is it an emotion. Intuition involves the very sophisticated process of taking complex bits of information and combining them in unique, complex ways. The process isn't invalidated just because you aren't consciously controlling it.

Recognizing Intuition

You can learn to recognize intuition and distinguish it from other less valid impressions you receive from time to time. Intuition is more the quality of a thought than an emotion. A thought might be quiet and vague at first, but it will *persist* until you either pay attention to it or you convince yourself that it is invalid. This quiet, persistent thought might be combined with a vague emotion or even a physical sensation, such as warmth or pressure. Sometimes we get fleeting impressions or confusing, mixed thoughts and feelings. These aren't intuition. Intuition wouldn't cause confusion unless you thought about it, doubted it, and analyzed it until you became confused. Extreme emotions, particularly fear, will not initially accompany intuition. They come only from trying to analyze it.

Analysis is best used on conscious thought processes. Unconscious thought processes typically require a longer, more laborious analysis than you have time to make when intuition is urging you to make a decision. Pay attention when you have a quiet, persistent thought giving you information or a vague impression. Try not to analyze it, judge it, or figure out where it came from. Instead, just try to be open to it, and listen to it, and see if it repeats.

If it does, heed what it tells you. It will not always make sense to you—it may not seem to fit with observable facts. Remember, intuition uses a lot more information than you have readily available to you on a conscious level. This information from the unconscious can influence the outcome of a decision in very significant ways, just as the more information you have changes and influences your conscious decisions. For example, you might decide to buy a car because you like its appearance. Then you might learn about some things that do not show on the surface, such as its gas mileage or how fast it will go or what the payments are. There are many things about situations and people that don't show on the surface at first.

We have all felt that little "nudge" at one time or another. Most people can happily point to instances when they followed their intuition and the results were good. Many of us can recall times when we did not pay attention to it and have regretted not following the guidance it gave.

When I completed my Ph.D. program in 1981, I was planning to move to my favorite city, start a psychology practice, and spend time with my fiancée and other friends. My plan seemed perfect. However, I kept having a thought that would not leave me alone. I kept thinking that I needed to take about six months off after a rigorous doctoral program and go somewhere to spend some time alone. I repeatedly ignored the thought because it made no sense to me. Why would I want to abandon such a perfect plan? And what of my fiancée? Surely I had to think of her happiness too!

I proceeded with my plans, not mentioning to anyone that I had a thought of doing anything else. I moved into a beautiful apartment on the waterfront, entertained my friends, enjoyed time with my fiancée, and began my practice.

Any new practice is a struggle, and mine was no exception. There were office procedures to define, and I faced a great deal of competition. Consequently, I needed to do a lot of public relations and marketing work as well as getting my practice set up. I was disturbed when I realized my partners weren't keeping most of the promises they had made to help me get started.

The situation became very stressful, especially after all the years of pressure and the demands of a graduate program. My eyesight began to fade. Tiny capillaries in my eyes broke and filled my eyes with blood, obstructing my vision.

This health problem incapacitated me so that I lost my practice, my fiancée, and my home. I realized that the persistent thought I'd had before, telling me I needed to take six months off—the thought I had ignored—was physical and intuitive guidance to help me avoid further tasking an already stressed body. I could have avoided the losses I sustained that year if I had listened to the guidance of my intuition.

On an unconscious level I knew my eyes had taken the brunt of the stress of the past few years. I also sensed there were certain untrustworthy characteristics in the people who were going to be my partners. My intuition made internal evaluations of those people, based on a basic knowledge of human nature, my past experiences with similar people, factors of the situation, and traits that these particular people portrayed. My intuition also had my past behavioral and physiological responses to draw from in determining and suggesting that I needed to take a six-month hiatus. Indeed, a long rest and relaxation period would have given my body and mind enough time to rejuvenate and prepare for the success and changes which then had to be postponed for many years. God had given me the guidance of intuition to help me avoid losses and to help me realize my dreams, but I ignored it.

Blocks to Intuition

What blocks us from recognizing and acting upon intuition? The main hindrance is our tendency to want conscious control of everything in our lives. In reality, we can have only partial control. When we accept this fact, we become freer to accept help from sources other than those we develop ourselves.

We also want to be able to explain everything in life. From the time we are two years old, we start asking "Why?" and expect answers. We grow up defending and justifying all our actions. But that we do not have all the answers is another fact of life. Seeking all the answers doesn't hurt us, but sometimes we need to have faith and accept help.

Fear can also block intuition. People are afraid of making the wrong decision, so they go with the one they can support with facts. There are people who are simply afraid of anything they cannot explain. What we fear is often what we don't understand, so learning to understand intuition can help ease any fear one might have about it.

The habit of always wanting to please people can interfere with your listening to your intuition. This will be an even stronger tendency for those who have such low self-esteem that they don't trust their own opinions and allow others to make decisions for them. People who work on acquiring a healthier self-esteem begin to trust their internal feedback and expect success. You will be right far more often if you listen and develop a sensitivity to your intuition. This is a form of guidance God has given you.

I once made a very important and successful career decision based on intuition. I had been invited to a psychology workshop on a subject in which I had already had much training and experience. The presenter was a well-known professional with whom I had worked during the previous year. I had tried persistently to befriend this colleague but he'd had no time for me. Consequently I didn't have a relationship with the presenter. For these reasons plus the fact that my schedule was already full, I planned to skip the workshop.

Two days before the workshop I had a severe twenty-four hour flu, which seemed to confirm my decision. I knew I wasn't going to feel like getting up early (I'm not a morning person, anyway) and driving through Southern California traffic to attend a workshop that I wasn't the least bit enthused about.

The morning of the workshop, however, I woke up early, feeling surprisingly well. I got in my car and drove down the Pacific Coast Highway, arguing with myself all the way. It seemed ridiculous! I was getting over the flu, I didn't want to sit through another lecture or participate in any learning exercises, and I couldn't think of anyone I particularly wanted to see there. But for some inexplicable reason, I felt I should go.

When I arrived, the leader was surprised and happy to see me. I sat through the lecture feeling a little spaced out from the antihistamines I was taking until the leader suddenly called on me to answer a question that had come up, saying, "Dr. Knippers is an expert in this area."

Well, I didn't hear the question, let alone know the answer, but I managed to get through it without looking too foolish. I stayed alert through the remainder of the workshop as he called upon me regularly to give my "expert" opinion.

During the lunch break, the leader happened to sit next to me and asked, "So, what's new with you, Chris?" I told him about a concept for a seminar I had been working on. I had actually been thinking about it for years but had only recently become serious about putting the plan into effect. It was a vision God had given me years earlier, and I was determined to fulfill it.

My colleague was more enthused about my seminar plans than I had ever seen him be enthused about anything before! He immediately volunteered to help me put the plan into action. He did, and it was a great success.

The seminar I developed was on listening to God's guidance. God helped make my vision a reality because I had followed the guidance He gave me to get out of my sick-bed, drive to another town early in the morning on my day off, and attend a workshop I had absolutely no interest in. It made no "sense" logically, but I have learned that when that quiet, persistent nudge comes, the only thing that does make sense, in the long run, is to do what it suggests. This type of guidance has never misdirected me.

The only "voices" that ever led me to make a wrong decision were voices of fear, doubt, and condemnation. If you hear a message that causes you to doubt your self-worth or that God wants anything but the best for your life in every way, or if you ever fear you cannot get through a problem you have, deny and defy that message with all the strength you can muster! Messages of fear, doubt, and condemnation are lies. Treat them as such.

Intuition will give you firm, definite messages along with a sense of confidence. Even a message warning you to avoid a situation or person will not have a sense of fear about it, just as the message that directed me away from my immediate post-graduate plans did not create fear concerning what I was about to do. Instead, the message prompted me in a positive direction to do something nurturing for myself.

God's guidance and nurturing are inherent in intuition. A good parent lovingly, confidently guides a child, and God is a good parent. His messages are loving and definite; they affirm our self-worth. Therefore, our intuition will always have safe, nurturing qualities.

Sometimes your intuition will direct you to seek a person or situation, just as mine prompted me to attend that workshop and talk to my colleague. Yours may guide you away from certain situations or people, just as mine told me to avoid that first practice I entered after finishing graduate school.

Your intuition won't condemn people, but it will give you a sense or message that a particular relationship isn't good for you. The person in question might be perfectly fine, but the context or timing of the relationship might be wrong for you. Perhaps something better awaits!

Your intuition, besides prompting you to approach something specific, will occasionally give you very general messages. For example, you might have a strong desire to take a drive, even though you don't have a specific destination in mind. This drive might lead you exactly where you need to go, or it might allow you to avoid some unpleasantness in the place you came from. Listen to even the general guidance of your intuition.

Many people use intuition habitually in one or a few aspects of their lives and ignore it in other areas. Some people, for example, use their intuition very effectively in business matters but not in personal relationships. We need to learn to listen to this God-given form of mental guidance to help us in *all* aspects of our lives.

Developing Your Intuition

You will become more sensitive to hearing your intuition and more accurate in discerning it as you have more experience with it. As you learn to detect the quality and types of messages that intuition brings and have success with it, the more confident you will be about making decisions based on it. Keeping a written account of your experiences will help you recognize sensitive, accurate intuition.

Start a journal and record the messages you believe came from your intuition. Write down your thoughts and feelings about these messages. Record whether you followed the guidance. Tell how you felt as and after you responded. Describe the outcome of the guidance and your response to it. Finally, write what you learned and gained from the outcome. You might find journaling is an enlightening experience that you will want to continue indefinitely. As you practice using your intuition and think about how it helps you, ultimately you will become much more accurate in your decision-making and much more effective in living!

Listen to the guidance that comes to you quietly, persistently, and gently, yet sometimes firmly. Listen to the messages that tell you to approach or to avoid, to move ahead, to stay where you are, or to go back. If you need validation of the messages your intuition gives you, ask the author of intuition—God—to guide you. He will let you know in some way if you are on the right track.

Becoming more aware of yourself through better awareness of your physical needs and emotional needs, the influence of your mind, and the feedback of your intuition will help you to be a more confident, secure person who helps others find what you have found.

THE
ULTIMATE SOURCE
OF GUIDANCE

W e have so many excellent sources of guidance available on a human level that it is easy to become arrogant and think we don't need to rely on anything or anyone other than ourselves and each other. The truth is even the common-sense feedback of the body, emotions, and mind, as well as the efficient insight of intuition, cannot tell us everything we need to know. At times we must transcend these human sources of guidance to receive the ultimate in guidance directly from God.

Each person experiences and hears God a little differently. That is why it is important for us to experience God individually. The prayers and spiritual insights of other people can be very helpful in our focusing in the right direction, but other people cannot give us exactly what we need spiritually. We must get our spiritual needs met through our own personal relationships with God.

We know that God is perfect love, perfect peace, perfect joy, and perfect insight. Beyond that is much more which cannot be put into words or is so personal only the individual can know it. Spending time with God will bring security, confidence, patience, insight, joy, peacefulness, and love to your life. The more time you spend with God, the more you will experience Him, and your own unique relationship with Him will develop.

We need God's presence to keep us focused on the truth. We must continually seek God to counteract the negative influences that can, at times, be so pervasive they distort our true perspectives. Even another person's mood can throw us off course without anyone consciously intending to send or receive such a communication. This is referred to as "mood contagion." Human behavior experts are working now to compile evidence of whether moods drift from one person to another via slight, unconscious signals, such as facial expressions, posture, and tone of voice. Dr. Elaine Hatfield, a University of Hawaii psychologist, told the *Los Angeles Times*: "A person is feeling something and showing it lots of different ways, and you find yourself feeling the same thing. That's what we mean by 'contagion.'"[1]

You might be experiencing other people's feelings rather than your own. You might even still be carrying the feelings or moods of the people with whom you grew up, even though you seldom or never see them. Many depressed people are actually just out of touch with their own feelings... their *positive* feelings. Very happy people can lose touch with their own happiness without even knowing it by becoming caught up in other people's discontent. You have nothing to fear or to be anxious about because God is available to you at all times. Keep in touch with the realities of *your* life by keeping in touch with God.

Before Christ left the earth in human form, He promised we would be able to do things even greater than He had done through God's Spirit dwelling within us and working through us. The Holy Spirit can fill a human life and provide supernatural guidance that is not available from any human source.

Obtaining this guidance is easy. Simply ask for it. God's Spirit is always available to communicate with us. When we feel we aren't communicating with God, it isn't because God has decided not to talk to us. It is because we are not open to receiving His Spirit and hearing Him. We don't pray to get God's attention, for we have it all the time. We pray to turn *our* attention to Him. If you want the Holy Spirit to guide you, simply turn your attention to God, and ask for guidance.

Some of my psychotherapy clients have presented me with seemingly hopeless problems and situations; yet my responsibility as their therapist is to help them find *some* option or at least to offer some hope. However, offering any hope I did not personally believe was genuine and practical would be very unethical. That is why I was so appalled when I found myself telling the desperate mother of a kidnapped twelve-year-old boy that everything was going to be all right. How did *I* know that? He was in New York with the Mafia!

Mrs. G. was a beautiful, thirty-six-year-old woman I had met at church. But the afternoon she came to my office, something had drastically altered her beauty. Her face was drawn and she had huge, dark circles under puffy eyes. She walked like a robot. She had been suffering from insomnia and loss of appetite. I listened in disbelief as she told her story.

Mr. and Mrs. G. and their two children had moved to Southern California from New York six years earlier. The marriage relationship had been strained in New York as they lived under the influence of his powerful, controlling family; but once they were in California, the marriage was transformed. The G. family was now relaxed, happy, and free. They had enough money so that it wasn't necessary for them to work. They were enjoying the Southern California lifestyle to the fullest.

A few weeks before Mrs. G. came to see me, her husband and son went to visit his family for a few days. Mrs. G. thought nothing of it. Taking a trip together to visit relatives sounded like a good idea for both father and son.

As the days passed, however, she thought it odd that her husband never called home. Eventually she called his parents' home. Mr. G.'s mother curtly told Mrs. G. that her husband and son were not there and hung up.

More days passed. Finally, about a week

after father and son should have returned to Southern California, Mr. G. phoned. He revealed that his family had always been involved in organized crime. Although he had fought being involved in it himself, the family had finally threatened to kill Mrs. G. if Mr. G. did not come back to New York and cooperate with "the family business." They had decided to keep the twelve-year-old son in order to train the boy for the role they wanted him to play in the future. Mr. G. warned his wife not to interfere in any way and then quickly hung up.

She was in shock for several days. As the reality of what had happened hit her, she cried continuously for days. She was unable to sleep or eat or take care of her six-year-old daughter.

Mrs. G. was not even sure what to ask of me. When I suggested that this was really a legal matter, she said she knew for a fact that Mr. G.'s family was involved in police departments across the nation and she believed they would have more influence in the judicial system than any attorney she could hire.

I looked at the broken woman, unable to function and sitting almost in a stupor before me, pleading for some kind of help. My heart broke as I looked at her, staring blankly at me. I fought back tears as I prayed silently for direction from the Holy Spirit.

Suddenly, words began to come from my mouth that I hadn't even thought of. Obviously it is always important to think carefully about the impact of what you are about to say to a client before you say it. And usually we have some thoughts about what we are going to say before we actually speak the words, but this time was an exception.

I told Mrs. G. that her son would return to her by himself before Thanksgiving (in approximately three weeks). She said, "How will he be able to get here? He has no money and is under constant guard!" I told her the boy would find an opportunity to slip away from the house when no one was looking. He would call a cab and go to the airport. There he would explain his situation to an airline agent. The airline would advance him a ticket, which Mrs. G. would pay for upon his arrival. I told her to expect her son to call her before Thanksgiving and say he was at Los Angeles International Airport. Mrs. G. accepted what I told her without comment. She brightened, thanked me, and left my office with a big smile.

I was stunned. I didn't know what to think.

Had the Holy Spirit really given those words to Mrs. G. through me or was I just desperately, selfishly trying to help her feel better and get her on her way? And why had she so readily accepted what I said as being absolutely true, to the last detail? Her whole countenance had changed after hearing those words.

I asked God to give me some insight into what had just happened. I felt assured that whatever had happened had been of God. I thanked Him for the miracle that was taking place and for allowing me to be part of it.

The Sunday after Thanksgiving, a radiant Mrs. G. and her handsome son greeted me at church. She said, "Everything happened exactly the way that you said it would. I went home from your office that day, ate a big meal, and slept for twelve hours. I have been praising God ever since. I knew it would all be a miracle. My husband has even called to assure me there will be no more trouble. His family voted to disown all of us and let us live separate lives."

I had no way of knowing any of what I told Mrs. G. My body and emotions certainly had no access to that kind of information. My conscious and unconscious mind had no access to details about the future of a child kidnapped by people with whom I'd had no experience. The most finely tuned intuition could not have instructed me about the destiny of this tragically troubled family. Yet the very words I spoke predicted the exact outcome of this complex situation. At that time, I'd had no experience with such phenomena. I'd done nothing more than pray a simple prayer because of a sincere desire to help this woman and comfort her. But through my prayer the Holy Spirit revealed the truth of a desperate situation.

The only way to know God's guidance is to ask for it. You are fully capable of receiving the ultimate guidance of the Holy Spirit in your life. You need only to ask sincerely for guidance, be open to receiving it, and be willing to follow it.

The guidance you receive may not come to you in the same way mine came to me. God has many ways to guide. Just be prepared to receive it once you've asked for it. If you need confirmation to know if the guidance you feel really is from God, again, just ask! God lets us know whether or not we are on the right track before it's too late.

Learning to recognize God's voice in your life helps you to know the source of true guidance.

CLEARING
THE BLOCKS TO
GOD'S GUIDANCE

God communicates with everyone all of the time. We just don't always hear. Our high-tech world pelts us with thousands of distractions that hinder us from hearing God. Our work, friends and family, recreation, entertainment, the news, advertising, and many other things bid daily for our attention. We need many of these "distractions" in order to function. We just don't need them all the time.

Internal distractions can be more subtle; the most destructive are guilt, fear, and anger. Others include unmet needs crying out for attention, unresolved emotional conflicts, and fatigue or "burn-out." We are often unaware of these internal distractions even though they can block us from hearing God's messages.

We need to keep the pathways of communication with God open wide. In order to do this we must first clear away whatever blocks His guidance.

Clearing External Blocks

You can clear your external blocks by taking time out of every day to relax your body and mind and just listen. You are much more open to hearing God when you are relaxed. When you relax, you may not be completely unaware of your thoughts, feelings, and the noise around you, but the more you tune out those distractions, the better you hear and experience God. The more you practice relaxation, the more you will be able to focus your attention on Him.

Relaxation can also aid the process of clearing internal blocks to God's guidance. Clearing away internal blocks can be a lengthy process and can require considerable effort and concentration. The rewards for your efforts will be well worth the energy you put into it!

Clearing Internal Blocks

The first half of this book dealt with getting certain human needs met by paying attention to the feedback provided by our bodies, minds, and emotions. This feedback and the needs that it represents are important by themselves, but there is another extremely important reason for us to get our human needs met. We are much more open to God when we are physically, mentally, and emotionally balanced. When we have strong unmet needs, those needs will demand our attention. Getting our needs met will make it easier for us to turn to and hear from God.

The world we live in, our genetic inheritances, and certain situations beyond our control make it difficult for us to be perfectly balanced in all areas of our lives all the time. You do not need to become consumed by a quest for the perfect balance of your human needs. That obsession would become another block! All you need to do is be aware of your needs; make whatever attempts you can to follow common-sense guidelines to get those needs met; then trust God with whatever you don't understand or whatever you perceive as being out of your own control. Chronic illnesses, both physical and emotional, can cause very troublesome imbalances. God's grace can overcome those imbalances, and God can still communicate with you, loudly and clearly.

Clearing Emotional Blocks

Guilt

Guilt is probably the most insidious of all the emotional blocks. After all, what was it that Christ sacrificed His life for? It was so we could be free from guilt! That is the basis for Christianity. One of the ironies of guilt is that it results from self-destructive behavior, but the guilt itself is as destructive as the behavior that caused it!

Guilt can also be caused by a misconception of ourselves or of our behavior. In other words, we don't actually have to commit a sin to destroy ourselves with guilt. We can just think we did something wrong or think we are just inherently inferior. These misconceptions start within the first six years of life, before we are even capable of understanding our feelings.

We don't have to have a religious background in order to feel guilt. Many authorities use guilt to manipulate children and adults, although they're not always aware they're doing it. Using guilt to control and manipulate is automatic for people who are filled with unconscious guilt themselves. Much of our society runs on manipulation by guilt tactics; advertising also uses subtle forms of guilt to get us to buy certain products and services.

We are not always aware of feeling guilt even when the unconscious mind is filled with it. The guilt from childhood misconceptions and from more subtle forms of manipulation we are exposed to daily fills our unconscious minds and poisons our everyday thoughts, feelings, behaviors, and interactions.

Guilt is often at the root of addictive behaviors. Unconscious guilt spills over into the conscious mind in the form of vague, uneasy feelings. We attempt to get rid of these feelings by engaging in some behavior to excess, which relieves the discomfort temporarily. After the relief wears off, the uneasy feelings return, accompanied by more guilt caused by the awareness that what we did to relieve our discomfort was excessive and destructive. Eventually, we return to the behavior that relieved the uneasy feelings before, and the cycle begins again.

Some behaviors we use to relieve stress may

be very good in and of themselves, but, practiced excessively, can be destructive. Work is an example of a "good" behavior which can become destructive if it is done in excess in order to avoid feelings.

Unconscious guilt can cause you to live with very uncomfortable situations: an unfulfilling job, a bad relationship, financial strain, health problems. Even people who do manage to have good things in life don't enjoy them if they have unconscious guilt.

If you find yourself repeatedly in the same uncomfortable situations, you are probably unconsciously sabotaging your conscious efforts to achieve good things. As mentioned earlier, the mind, particularly the unconscious, has tremendous influence on your life. You can actually make your life an exercise in punishment just because you carry misconceptions about your self-worth or something you did or did not do. You may repeatedly ask for God's forgiveness but not fully accept it due to unconscious guilt.

We are actually capable of structuring our lives around unconscious guilt. We ignore opportunities for happiness and success, push away people who would be good for us, and make ourselves sick if we have conscious or unconscious guilt.

That was the story of my life. I tried everything to rid myself of guilt: legalistic religion, hedonism, liberal religion, psychotherapy, and various radical medical treatments. Psychotherapy helped rid me of much conscious guilt. At that point, I thought my life would be completely successful. I was indeed much happier, but I still faced many uncomfortable situations, such as poor health and inadequate finances. In my daily sessions of listening to God, I asked for insight into my problem. It came to me that the problem was unconscious guilt. I asked if it was due to anything I had done wrong in the past. God assured me my past was forgiven. I asked if I was currently doing anything for which I needed forgiveness. God assured me there would always be room for improvement in my behavior, but my current shortcomings were not the cause of my unconsciously structuring my life so I was always uncomfortable. Unconscious guilt caused by old misconceptions of myself and my behavior blocked me from receiving all the blessings I was working so hard for. Some time in my past I had gotten the idea I was a "bad" person. The idea became deeply ingrained even though with my logical thought processes I could not think of why.

I began spending daily, half-hour sessions with God for the express purpose of allowing God to cleanse me of all guilt past or present, real or imagined. After many weeks of these daily cleansing sessions, I began to notice that my health, finances, career, and relationships were all improving significantly!

Relax in God's presence. Ask God to reveal to you the sources of your guilt. Be honest with yourself and God. Share the results of these sessions with a supportive, nonjudgmental person. Ask God to help you eliminate all the sources of guilt you can. There will be some things that you, on your own power, will not be able to do away with. Let God take those things and handle them in His own way and time. Picture God flooding your body, mind, and spirit with the light of Christ's forgiveness. Then relax in everything you do, knowing you are forgiven, guided, and filled with grace.

Freedom from guilt will allow you to receive the blessings God wants to bring into your life: fulfilling activities, loving relationships, personal peace, and fulfillment of your needs. Best of all, you will have clear communication with God.

Fear

Fear is another major block to clear communication with God. Fear can influence us in ways that are just as negative and self-destructive as guilt. Fear can prevent you from taking chances or going against the established order of things, even when doing so would make you more successful and fulfilled within God's will. Fear keeps people in damaging relationships because they are insecure about being alone and feel that even a harmful relationship is better than none. Unconscious fears can block you from ever seeing obvious opportunities for greater fulfillment.

You probably had real reasons to have fear at one time in your life. The world can be a genuinely frightening place both when you're a child and an adult. Even though we learn defenses and that God and some people can be trusted, we might still have vague or unconscious fears left over from negative experiences. Guilt can produce the fear of being punished.

The greatest way to overcome fear is to learn to trust in and communicate with God. When you know that God is always available to give you the most accurate guidance, you become very secure. You are constantly aware of the fact that you can make the right decisions and be in the right place and with the right people at the right time based upon your communication with God.

It is also extremely helpful to routinely make positive statements to yourself concerning your own protection and safety. It's easy to slip back into insecurity. Keep reminding yourself of the truth: You are protected, safe, secure, guided by God, and you are capable of doing anything you really need to do!

Anger

Although anger is healthy, unresolved anger can block your communication with God. Anger can be a positive force that motivates us to make needed changes in our lives and helps us to confront people and situations that must be dealt with. When we don't express and release our anger in a healthy way, it can lodge in our conscious or unconscious minds. There it can grow and mix with other emotions to produce something much stronger than the original healthy anger. Unresolved anger can erupt at unexpected times. It can cause us to overreact to people and situations. We might say things we regret. Anger can control us and destroy good relationships.

When emotions control us, God can't. We need to be in control of what we say and do so we can hand over control to God.

The anger that becomes stuck in our minds was at one time appropriate. Perhaps you were not allowed or were afraid to express your anger at the time. You might have been taught that anger is a sin. Some of us had poor examples of how to express anger; one or both parents might have had uncontrolled, frightening fits of rage. Therefore, you associated those fearful experiences with expressing anger and decided to never act that way. When you do that, you repress your anger. But anger will not stay repressed for long.

Some people don't know that they are expressing anger, and they might fool you too. They can say insulting things so subtly, and with such big smiles on their faces, you may never know what hit you. But the effect is the same as if you had been blatantly insulted. In fact, the effect of a passive attack can be worse than a direct attack. At least with a direct attack, you can defend yourself. These passive attacks can go directly into your unconscious and negatively affect your self-esteem.

Sometimes we hold onto anger as a defense against being hurt again. The anger prevents us from becoming close to the person who hurt us; therefore, we won't risk feeling pain again. Anger becomes a shield we're afraid to let go of for fear of being vulnerable. The truth is that this unresolved anger causes more damage than we risk by being vulnerable. This is why confrontation, forgiveness, and releasing anger is so important. These tools free us from the destruction anger can cause in our relationships, our bodies, and even our careers. When you have communication with God and with your human sources of feedback, such as intuition, you don't need as many defenses. You know when to risk and when not to.

The healthiest way to handle your anger is to express it as soon after it occurs as possible. Still, it is always best to have a brief "cooling off" period before confronting someone. Tell him or her, without insult, what bothered you. Then drop it. After confrontation, it is important to forgive and to realize this can work toward good results in your life. Release your anger, and the person or situation that caused it, to God. You will begin to feel peaceful and confident.

If your anger has already been repressed or stuck in your mind, you need to try to remember its source as much as possible, express it if you feel you need to, forgive those involved, and forgive yourself for everything you have gotten angry at yourself about. You will find that you are much happier.

General Guidelines for Dealing with Unresolved Emotions

- Relax your body and mind. Pray and listen for guidance in understanding the problem and finding solutions to troublesome emotions.
- Look at your past to understand where and how your unresolved emotion began.
- Look at your present life to realize you are in control of how you handle your current and past emotions and situations.
- Forgive people and incidents of the past and practice healthy ways of responding to your present feelings and situations. Forgive *yourself* for any real or perceived shortcomings.
- Look at your future to see if you like where you are headed. (People become insecure and angry about a possible future they don't like.)

- Take responsibility for your future by changing directions, doing something different, or taking more chances if you want to go in a different direction with your life.
- Surrender everything about your life to God.

Surrender

The most freeing step you can take in clearing the blocks from your life is to surrender everything in your life to God. Surrender is actually an attitude. It says you completely trust that God is taking perfect control of your life—past, present, and future—and you are staying in contact with Him for continual direction of your thoughts, feelings, and actions.

Once you have developed the attitude of surrender, you are free to live a joyful, secure, satisfying life, resting in the assurance that you are living God's perfect will for you. In this state, you are constantly open to receiving God's love, communication, and blessing.

Prepare to receive! Look for God's presence in every area of your life. You will find it.

Developing Trust

In order to surrender, you need to trust God, but trust is difficult for many people. It might require some practice.

One way to practice trusting God is to repeat statements of truth about God to yourself throughout the day. Try the following:

- God loves and accepts me.
- God wants me to be healthy, happy, and fulfilled.
- God can work miracles in and through my life.
- I can trust God completely.
- "Christ gives me the strength to face anything" (Phil. 4:13 CEV).
- "God's Spirit does not make cowards out of us. The Spirit gives us power, love and self-control" (2 Tim. 1:7 CEV).
- "Now glory be to God who by his mighty power at work within us is able to do far more than we would ever dare to ask or even dream of—infinitely beyond our highest prayers, desires, thoughts, or hopes" (Eph. 3:20 TLB).

Another way to practice trust is to close your eyes and picture yourself in the presence of Christ, handing over each part of your life to Him—career, relationships, health, finances. Do this until you are comfortable seeing those areas of your life taken over by God.

Trust in God builds when you remember all the times in your life when He has rescued you. You might have been in a life-threatening situation or condition or had financial trouble. Somehow you survived those problems. Something brought you out of your darkest hour. Avoid the tendency to think you were just "lucky," forgetting how distressed you really were.

God has worked miracles in your life, and some of them you are unaware of. Your trust in God will be boosted if you remember all the times you were saved from problems. It was God who saved you. Write down as many of your past problems as you can remember; then remember how you got out of them. Give credit to God for bringing about solutions to those problems.

With trust in God, you will be more able to hear God and more open to the different ways in which God communicates with you.

DISCERNING GOD'S VOICE FROM THE OTHERS

We are bombarded with voices all the time. They come from every direction, trying to influence you to do this, buy that, go here, stay there. People try to enlist your help personally and through the media. If your goals conflict with what others want to accomplish, they will try to move you out of the way. That is human nature. It is understandable that we would have so many different influences vying for our attention.

With all of this "noise" in our lives, distinguishing God's voice from the others can be difficult. But God's communication has distinguishing characteristics. When you are aware of some of these, you can tell the difference between God's voice and those of social pressure, your own emotions, career or power ambition, prejudice, and so on.

Distinguishing Characteristics

God communicates with us through many different means: people, thoughts, memories, an audible voice, visions, songs, the arts, entertainment, reading, serendipity, and angels. Whatever the means, the characteristics of God's messages are similar.

God tries to get our attention in ways that are pleasant to us. If the pleasant ways don't work, He might use less likable methods. Knowing the ways God communicates will help you recognize when He is speaking to you so you can pay attention!

Direct communication from God is different in content from communication from our internal, human sources of feedback like intuition. Intuition can draw upon forgotten thoughts and experiences, but communication from God can draw upon any information, whether or not we have had any experience with it. God can tell you things you need to do based on things that are going to happen in your future. God doesn't tell everyone specifics about the future. That is a special type of communication from God, and is a spiritual gift only certain people have. Actually preparing for your future requires more faith if you don't know exactly what it holds.

Sometimes we ignore God's messages. Then we wonder why our lives don't seem to be going in the right direction or sometimes any direction.

Obviously the content of God's messages may seem a bit strange at times. Occasionally you are going to look like an idiot to other people if you listen to and do what God tells you. Develop a sense of humor about yourself and your critics. Just remember that you will look even worse if you don't do what God tells you to do! You don't always have to know the beginning from the end. What you really need to know, God will tell you. Most of the time, it's really best to not know the future. If we did, most of us would try to take control of it and really mess things up!

The messages God gives us have a sense of *authority*. Your initial impression will be that this message is important. The communication has a certain strength. The Bible refers to God's voice as a "still, small voice" which is strong and authoritative. When you have the impression that the communication you receive through thought, desire, experience, or other means has the "sound" of authority or strength to it, pay attention, and ask God for confirmation of its source.

A sense of *peace* is part of a communication that comes from God. Even when the message is one we would rather not hear, we can accept it peacefully. If a message really disturbs you, it is probably from a source other than God.

Fear is never of God. A strong sense of fear accompanying a message is an indication the message comes from somewhere other than God. "God has not given us a spirit of fear, but of power and of love and of a sound mind" (2 Tim. 1:7). Peace is of God. Listen to the voice of authority and peace.

God has ultimate *respect* for you. You are God's prized creation. Any message to you from God will show this. There will never be a condemnation or any kind of "put-down." Your Creator loves you unconditionally, and that will always be evident in the communication He gives to you. God might say *no* when you were hoping for *yes*. He might want you to stop when you want to go, but there will never be even a hint of disrespect for you. Listen to the voice of authority, peace, and respect.

Trust God with your future. Listen when you have urges to do something that makes no sense. Ask God for guidance as to whether to pay attention to those urges. If they are of God, the messages will persist and likely will become clearer. You will also probably become more comfortable with what you are hearing and being told to do. Then do it!

The content of God's messages can be mysterious, unique, even "illogical," but they are always clear. You will find that God is not limited to one medium for sending you messages. There are many sources of God's communication to you. He is unlimited.

The Media for God's Messages

The following are a few examples of how God communicates with us through different means.

Certain *thoughts* will get your attention either by content or by the way they arrive (for example, you have them suddenly or upon waking they are in your mind). A profound thought might come to you during a boring or routine activity. The timing of the thought could be significant. It might be repetitious.

When you have such thoughts, pray and think or meditate about them. Write them down. As you are led to do so, act on the information you received from the thought. Thoughts God gives you will be persistent, consistent, and firm.

Your *memories* sometimes come back to give you a word from God. Thoughts, experiences, and words from the past can make more sense in the present. When a long-forgotten memory comes back to you, pay attention to it. It could be an important clue or message from God regarding something you have been seeking or something you are to seek.

God's communications are often delivered to us through *other people's words*. A friend might say something, knowingly or unknowingly, that stands out significantly to you. You might hear a speech or a sermon that has a message directly for you. Overhearing a stranger's conversation can deliver a word you need to hear. Any form of human speech can be a means of your getting a message from God.

A few years ago I knew I was feeling healthy, but I wondered if my life span would be normal. My body had endured great strain with diabetes and other problems. I asked God for a sign concerning how much time I could expect to have to fulfill the work He wanted me to do. The next day a stranger walked up to me at church and said, "I am seventy-one years old, and have had diabetes all my life. I am perfectly healthy. You, too, are going to live a long and healthy life." She then disappeared into the crowd. God gave me an answer through a stranger. I am thankful she listened to God and acted on what He told her. Now I have the assurance that I have plenty of time to do the work God has given me.

People's actions can give us insight into something God wants us to know or do. You might be impressed by a single act you witness another person doing, or you might be impressed with that person's life in general. If you find another person's behavior gets your attention in a positive way, there could be something for you to learn from that person which would help you fulfill God's will for your life.

Reading the words of other people can also deliver very important messages. Many books have made me feel totally affirmed and good about myself in only a few minutes, even though for years friends and family had tried but could not convince me of my worth. Other books have inspired me to change my whole view of the world. An article, a brief devotional, or even a clever saying scribbled on a piece of paper can be the means God uses to deliver profound messages. Even reading your own words from a journal you wrote earlier can make something very clear to you.

God has changed my life through the things I was led to say in this book. Write down the thoughts and experiences you believe are from God. You can learn valuable truths from the things you write.

A dramatic *experience* can illustrate God's truth. Being saved from a traffic accident, witnessing a miracle, experiencing childbirth, going through a storm, an illness, or a healing, running into an old friend, sensing a spiritual presence. . . . Any number of experiences, both common and uncommon, can bring God's communication to us. When the ordinary events of life spontaneously take on special meaning for us, or give us personal revelations, those experiences are referred to as *serendipities*.

Once, when I needed a real boost to my faith and was feeling all alone in the world, I asked God to reveal His presence. At that moment, three hummingbirds appeared outside my window and stayed suspended there, looking in at me, for almost twenty minutes. Those birds took on deep, spiritual meaning for me. God is always trying to get our attention in any way He can. Look for God in the experiences of your life.

Nature can inspire us and show us certain aspects of God's character. We can see illustrations of God in all that was created. We can see God working, right before our eyes, when we pay attention to nature. Nature is like a huge classroom for learning God's truth. Take every opportunity you can to learn about God and from God in the great laboratory of His universe.

Paintings, plays, songs, operas, films, symphonies, and other products of God-inspired creativity have given thousands of people inspiration and revelation through the centuries. True creativity is a gift of God. Some of these inspired works might appear to be entirely secular, yet carry a spiritual message to the individual listener/viewer.

Several years ago, I was asked to speak at a very prestigious event. I was shocked but delighted that I had been asked to appear on such an important platform. I felt unworthy and unprepared, but it was an opportunity I thought I needed to take.

In the next several weeks, I tried to pump up my confidence and prepare what I would say. By the time the morning of the speech arrived, my words were ready but I wasn't. I lay down on my living room floor before leaving the house and asked God for confidence. Immediately I felt a desire to turn on the radio. I often used music as a means to relax, but that wasn't what I thought I needed right then. I followed the prompt anyway because I believed it was from God.

The radio happened to be tuned to a rock station I rarely listened to. As soon as I turned it on, this song played and changed my life forever:

> Know who you are.
> There's a world wants to know you.
> Know where to go.
> There's a world wants to touch you.
> Feel all you can.
> Let your heart speak and guide you.
> Don't be afraid of the love deep inside you.
> Bring it out for everyone.
> When you smile we can see the sun.
> Bring it out for all to hear,
> Because you've so much to give,
> And there's so much to know.
> But if you wait for your moment,
> Well, it may never show.

Know who you are.
There's a new song inside you.
Weep if you can.
Let the tears fall behind you.
Bring it out for everyone.
When you smile we can see the sun.
Sing it out for all to hear,
Because you've so much to say,
And you've so much to do,
And everyone's waiting.
Yes, it's all up to you.

Know who you are.
There's a world deep inside you.
Trust if you can.
There's a friend there to guide you. [1]

This song was a direct message from God. It was an affirmation and a command to go to that speaking engagement with the confidence that He had given me a message to deliver and He would guide me and shine through me.

I delivered the speech with such enthusiasm that afterward I was almost mobbed by people, wanting to express their gratitude for the way it had inspired them.

God can use some very unexpected means to deliver guidance to us.

As described in the Bible, sometimes God communicates His messages to us in *dreams*.

Dreams can be simply a release of repressed emotions, a rehearsal of events of the day, or the acting out of a wish. But they can also carry important messages. When you wake with a dream on your mind, especially if the dream was vivid, write it down, pray for the correct interpretation to come to you, and attempt to find a message in it. If a possible interpretation comes to you, write that down. If a satisfactory interpretation does not come, put the dream aside, and ask God for further direction. If there is a message, God will make sure you get it through another dream or another means. There is no need to strain at finding hidden meanings. God will persist in getting through to you if you are sincere in seeking His will.

Many quite sane people actually hear an *audible voice* when God speaks to them. I've heard God's voice audibly only one time that I can remember. I was praying silently one night at bedtime. I had just asked for His help with a problem, when a distinct voice spoke into my right ear and said, "You do not have a problem."

I jumped up, opened my eyes, and said, "God, is that You?"

Again, the voice said, "You do not have a problem."

I have not heard that voice since, but those words came into my thoughts about once a year as over time I prayed about that "problem." Eventually I learned I didn't have a problem!

I can't describe exactly what God's voice sounded like except to say it was calm, distinct, and clear. We all seem to hear God's voice differently.

Since the beginning of time, *angels* have been God's messengers. Thousands of accounts of angelic intervention are in the ancient and modern writings of highly respectable people, including the Reverend Billy Graham.

We believe angels are actual beings, similar in some ways to humans. They are able to carry out specific functions for God in the heavenly and earthly realms. While you and I are capable of serving God in our unique ways on earth, angels are capable of traveling between realms. I believe they are working in our world in people's personal lives, routinely and constantly, without our slightest awareness. But occasionally people are aware of having had a brush with an angel.

I have heard several accounts similar to the one my friends Dan and Sherry had. They were stranded by car trouble in the middle of a desert. After two hot hours when no one came into sight and they had no way to fix the car or get to a phone, a stranger called out to them from behind where they were standing. He offered to help. Evidently he had walked across the desert, because he had no car. He told them to sit on the back of their car and relax.

They were skeptical but had little choice other than to trust him and hope for the best. In five minutes, he had the car running. Dan and Sherry stared at the functioning engine in amazement. When they turned toward the stranger to thank him, no one was in sight. They drove up and down the highway trying to find him, but the desert was just as barren and lifeless as it had been when they prayed alone for two hours in the stifling heat. Dan is a very logical accountant and Sherry is an engineer. I have never known either of them to dramatize or exaggerate anything. They are careful who they tell this story to, but every time they tell it, they praise God for sending an angel to help them.

The angel who helped Dan and Sherry looked quite human. That isn't always true, for I once met an angel who appeared in a very ethereal form. I had just been given the diagnosis that I was going blind. I was so distraught I was actually planning my suicide. I had even told my family of my decision to prepare them for the shock.

At that time, I lived alone in an apartment with no windows in the bedroom, so it was always very dark at night. This particular night I was awakened by a soft glow from across the bedroom. A beautiful woman with long, glowing hair and wearing a long, flowing gown was sitting sideways on my desk chair. Both she and her gown were translucent light.

As I raised up to get a closer look, she remained motionless, looking directly at me. I decided to go into the dressing room, turn on the bright lights, and splash cold water on my face. I thought I really needed to wake up. She continued watching me as I walked past her.

When I was sure I was awake, I went back into the bedroom. She was still sitting on my desk chair and still looking at me. I went back to my bed, lay down, and turned to face her. I fell asleep watching her loving face. Her presence and gentle gaze assured me that I was loved, valued, and safe. From that moment forward, I never had another suicidal thought. I determined to live and overcome any adversity I might face in the future.

As you listen for the distinguishing characteristics of God's voice in the midst of all the
other voices in your life, remember that God uses
many ways to communicate His messages.

KNOWING GOD'S WILL FOR YOU

We learn to use our common sense, intuition, and God's guidance in order to accomplish His will in our lives. The New Testament tells us not to be conformed to the world, but to be transformed by the renewing of our minds so that we can find the good, acceptable, perfect will of God for us. Romans 12:2 tells us not to go along with whatever society dictates to us, but to use our minds to discover what God wants us to do with our lives.

We each have vital functions to perform according to God's will for the world. You are an essential part of God's plan for the universe. He wants to use you to impact others.

Doing God's will does not require any special human power, but only a willingness to allow His power to flow through you. Often people say they are afraid to give their lives to God because they fear they will disappoint Him. The truth is God created you with the ability to do whatever He wants you to do. As you learn to know His will through using your common sense and intuition, and by following His guidance, you can begin to fulfill His marvelous plan to impact the world.

God's General Plan

God has both general and specific plans for the world. Christ taught us about God's will for humanity, saying, "For God so loved the world that He gave His only begotten Son, that whoever believes in Him should not perish but have everlasting life. For God did not send His Son into the world to condemn the world, but that the world through Him might be saved" (John 3:16-17). God wants each of us to live securely and vitally, with the knowledge that He has saved us from ultimate destruction.

Because of our salvation, we are part of revealing the good news of the Gospel of Jesus

Christ to other people. We are all part of God's plan to offer His supernatural, unconditional love to everyone in the world. That is the general plan, and there are more specific things God wants you to have in your life, as well, that He wants you to share with others.

Love

The first is the "golden rule," of loving others in the way you should yourself. Note that loving yourself precedes loving others. We must be more patient, kind, gentle, understanding, and nurturing with ourselves before we can effectively love other people. We need to take care of our own emotional and physical needs and not criticize ourselves when we make mistakes. Instead we need to have compassion on and comfort ourselves with our knowledge of God's forgiveness.

Notice the thoughts you have toward yourself, especially when you make a mistake and when you accomplish something good, remembering that your thoughts determine how you behave. Are you patient when you make a mistake? You need to be. Are you happy when you accomplish something good? You need to be.

Remember, you treat others the way you treat yourself.

Loving others as we love ourselves keeps us from becoming either too self-centered or too self-exploiting. God wills that we have a healthy balance in our lives.

Power

"For God has not given us a spirit of fear, but of power and of love and of a sound mind" (2 Tim. 1:7). Anything that contradicts a sense of power in you is not of God and is not His will for you. God is all-powerful, and His power is available to you.

Look at the earthly life and works of Jesus Christ. Before He left this earth, He told us we would be able to do even greater things than He had done. What power! It is important to keep in mind the source of that power—it's not human. All power comes from God. Knowing Him will give you tremendous confidence.

Health

Undoubtedly, health is one of the primary foci of Christ's ministry; look at the many biblical accounts of healing. It was never conditional. All that the supplicant needed was to believe it could be done! Seek health for yourself, and God will provide whatever you need to have the physical health He wants for you.

Thank God, every day, for your health, and keep seeking health, regardless of your current condition. You will find whatever you need to do God's will and to help others find healing. And remember, no one has the right to judge your relationship with God according to how healthy you are.

Your emotional health is also a part of God's will for you. Christ said, "He has sent Me to heal the brokenhearted" (Luke 4:18). Our emotional conditions can become broken no matter how spiritual we are. That is part of being human. God provides healing for that brokenness. Seek healing for yourself in relationships with God and supportive people, and then search out other people for whom your love can provide healing.

Spiritual Gifts

The Bible instructs us to have hope, faith, and trust because they are essential to a fulfilling life. We find these in the same ways that we come to know God and His unconditional love. We need to spend time in God's presence to experience faith, hope, and trust, and we need to be familiar with the qualities of thought and behavior that reflect them. God's will is that we will have these qualities and help others find them too.

Hope is the expectation of something you desire in your life. This expectation builds tremendous endurance, even when there is little or no evidence the desire will be fulfilled.

"Faith is the substance of things hoped for, the evidence of things not seen" (Heb. 11:1); faith is a very strong belief. The more you spend time with God and exercise your hope, the more your faith will develop. You will learn that your hopes can become realities, and your faith will increase. It will be contagious.

"Trust in the LORD with all your heart, and lean not on your own understanding" (Prov. 3:5). This Scripture confirms that God wills us to trust Him and not place all our hope in human logic. It is difficult for many to do this. We think we should have proof for everything we believe and should trust only provable scientific theories, particularly in higher education. However, the scientific processes are frequently irrelevant to our knowing how to manage our daily lives. We must trust when we believe God is telling us to do something. He will be patient with you as you question and as you proceed slowly toward doing the thing He is telling you to do, so long as you are making some movement in the right direction.

It is important to separate trust in humans from trust in God, for humans can be trusted only conditionally. We are all going to disappoint each other at times. I often meet people who won't trust God because they have been betrayed, repeatedly, in human relationships. But God's trustworthiness is on a completely different level. Learn the degree to which you can trust the people in your life; forgive them when they fall short, and expect them to improve. Place your full trust in God; He never falls short.

Abundance

Christ said, "I have come that they may have life, and that they may have it more abundantly" (John 10:10). God's will is that we will have an abundance of the best His creation offers: loving relationships, health, joy, peace, and a beautiful environment.

Many people believe the Scriptures also refer to financial prosperity when they reveal God's perfect plan for us. The author of Third John wrote, "I pray that you may prosper in all things and be in health, just as your soul prospers" (3 John 2). The author appears to distinguish between spiritual and material prosperity in this verse and gives both importance. We do need to prosper at least enough so that the emotional and physical stresses resulting from a lack of the necessities of life won't hamper our relationships with God and others. What we know, affirmatively, is that it is God's will for us to experience the best life has to offer.

Positive Influence on Others

We have a degree of influence on everyone we meet. Do you realize that people look to you for some measure of how life should be lived? We have all experienced insecurity and tried to hide it. Most insecure people have learned to effectively mask their insecurities by compensating with their strongest traits. A person might use her intellectual "superiority" to appear secure, or a physically attractive person might hide behind his appearance.

You never know for whom you might be a role model, especially if someone perceives you as being more secure than he or she is. In a seminar I attended, Dr. Scott Peck, psychiatrist and author of *The Road Less Traveled*, said we are all always using our influence to either heal or teach, whether we know it or not. It is God's will that we use our influence on other people to heal and teach them in the best ways possible through our acts of love.

Paying attention to the influences other people have on you and using their influence for the good is also important. As a psychotherapist, I am aware that everyone I counsel can help me as I help them. Psychotherapy is a process in which a therapist and client allow God to enter their lives and heal both of them.

Allow others to have a healing influence on you by discovering the good in everyone you meet. Whether it is your father, mother, spouse, child, friend, boss, co-worker, employee, arch rival, or a complete stranger, discover the worth of the other people in your life. In the process, you will enhance your own and influence others positively.

Jan's story reveals how following common sense, intuition, and God's guidance can bring you into the fulfilling will of God.

Jan was afraid to do anything meaningful with her life even though she was financially secure, had a graduate degree in psychology, and had excellent health. Her two sons were adults and independent. She lived in a fine house, paid for by her former husband. These two former spouses lived independent lives in separate wings of the house, even though they had been divorced for over five years.

Jan was a devout Christian, but her life seemed empty. She spent much time alone. She read, went to church, and occasionally had lunch with a friend. She was an intelligent, educated, healthy, forty-two-year-old woman who lived without close relationships, a career, or even a hobby.

Jan finally began to admit she felt her life no longer had purpose. Until about six years earlier, she had worked full-time, volunteered for charitable work, and was active socially and in her children's lives. Her life was full and productive; or was it? If it had been so wonderful, why did she retreat behind the walls of her ex-husband's home into a pseudo-relationship that had long since ended emotionally, and withdraw from all other relationships and activities? Why had she dropped out of life? We began to explore these questions.

Jan had indeed lived a very busy life. Not only had she worked to make money for her family, she had also worked to make peace and happiness for them. She had spent all her energy on her husband and children and anyone else who asked for her attention.

What's wrong with this picture?

Despite Jan's tireless efforts to save the lives of her alcoholic husband, her troubled sons, and the people of her church, her husband was jailed for repeated DUI offenses, one son ran away from home with a motorcycle gang, the other son became very depressed, and the people of her church kicked her out for getting a divorce. At that point Jan, too, judged herself a total failure. In fact, she believed she was a curse. She thought her efforts to save everyone in her life were not only completely futile, but actually damaging. She decided to get out of everyone's way, keep a low profile, and not do anything for fear she would do the wrong thing.

Jan had lived her entire life without getting her own needs met. As a result, she burned out, and ended up being almost useless even to herself. As we sorted through the events and feelings of her life, we explored how all her efforts had made a difference in people's lives, and how the choices that other people had made were not her responsibility. She had gone beyond the call of duty to give them better alternatives and opportunities, but they had made the decisions that brought them their trouble. It was now time, though, for Jan to get her needs met!

We began with helping Jan recognize her emotional-psychological needs, give them credibility, and learn how to fulfill them. This was a long process because it was such a foreign concept to Jan.

We also began helping Jan trust her own intuition. This was less difficult, as Jan was experienced in the positive outcome of following this form of guidance.

When it came time to work on Jan's need for purpose, this meant finding God's will. After so many years of discounting her own self-worth and having others confirm her opinion, I knew that it was going to be difficult for Jan to believe she was capable of doing anything God wanted her to do. I also knew I was not going to be able to completely convince her that she had what it takes to succeed; but I knew who could.

I told Jan to spend at least a half hour every day in a physically and mentally relaxed state, just listening to God. She focused on all of God's unconditional love for her. The more love she experienced, the more capable she felt.

I asked her to listen with her mind for any messages she sensed might be coming to her from God during or after these sessions of listening, and she wrote these communications in a journal. We called it her "Truth Journal" because she was to accept this as the absolute truth about herself and her life.

The truths that came to Jan transformed her. She began to realize her own self-worth and how wrong the human influences in her life had been about her. She forgave and felt compassion for all of those who had betrayed, rejected, and abused her. Jan became the most energetic, confident, compassionate woman I could ever hope to meet.

God directed Jan to use her education and her practical experience to help children who had been abused and molested. She began leading a special outreach that has touched thousands of lives, bringing little souls into the presence of a loving God who can be the perfect parent.

Truth Journal

You can listen to God and find the peace, purpose, confidence, and joy that Jan and many men and women have found. Keeping a journal of your experiences in communion with God will help you focus on His love for you and discover ways you can give it to others.

Take at least twenty minutes a day to relax, using the methods you've learned in previous chapters. When you are relaxed, think about the specific qualities of God's unconditional love: He is patient, kind, positive, unfailing, persevering, hopeful, forgiving, strong. Imagine God seeing you just as you are now and as you have been in the past, and loving you unconditionally.

Then throughout each day, write down any messages you believe are from God. As we have seen, He speaks through a variety of means. You will find His communication to you becoming more and more clear as you continue your journal. This journal will become your reference for truth in your life, especially when events, circumstances, and negative people challenge every hope you have! You can always go to your journal and hear again the words God spoke to you. You will find that God's words do come true as you dwell on them and believe them. His affirmation will help you know and accomplish His fulfilling will for you.

CHAPTER 9

PLANS OF ACTION

This book contains many suggestions about how to receive all of the direction and guidance that will make your life fulfilling. Some people will want to improve their lives in all of the areas dealt with in this book, while others will want to focus on only one or a few areas. I suggest taking one at a time in the beginning. Begin with prayer for guidance in the area of life that you are working on, move on to consciously relaxing your body and mind; then, wait for guidance to come to you. You'll be aware of specific direction at the time of your prayer and listening and/or afterward.

Some people will need to spend a week, focusing twice daily for twenty minutes a session, before they notice results in a particular area. Others will need to spend months. Still others will notice changes in their lives immediately. After making a connection with physical, emotional, mental, and spiritual forms of guidance, maintain that connection with daily prayer and listening sessions.

Seeking the help of professionals with whom you feel comfortable is always a good idea. Try to find someone you trust to refer you. Then, pay attention to how you feel with that person. Your life is very important, and you need to feel comfortable with the person who is going to help guide your life.

Feel free to ask questions of your chosen professional. A professional who is open about him- or herself and takes time to answer your questions is probably a good choice. Try to find professionals who value their own time enough to charge for their services, yet are flexible in their fees or payment plans. In addition, try to find out how this person spends free time. Because of the intensity of their work, professionals have a tendency to become burned out. You want someone who is balanced in his or her activities and does not appear to be overworked.

Make sure you are the center of attention for any services you pay for. A person who can share from his or her own life experiences, without dominating the session with personal stories or concerns, is preferable. You are not necessarily looking for someone who "has it all together," but you do want someone who can relate to what you are going through and is at least a few steps ahead of you. It is also good to go to someone who admits he or she doesn't have all the answers and encourages you to participate in determining what is best for you.

Regardless of whether or not you decide to go to a professional, you are responsible for seeking the guidance you have available to you. You are responsible for following it and for maintaining that connection. It is possible to lose the connection even after receiving guidance and direction for a long period of time. We are very easily distracted and susceptible to going into denial. Daily maintenance of your two-way communication with God is essential.

Prayers for Guidance

To help you maintain this connection, you can record the following prayers in your own voice and play them during relaxation sessions. This is a highly effective way to relax and walk through the processes outlined in the prayers. Move slowly through them, especially during the relaxation portion. Be sure to pause for at lease five minutes where the prayers call for reflection, recalling, or listening. These prayers will bring clarity in your life.

God bless you on your journey!

Physical Guidance

Dear God,

I thank You that I am fearfully and wonderfully made in Your image. I know You want the best health possible for me. Please guide my mind, emotions, and spirit as I seek to hear from this miraculous body You created. Help me to relax every muscle of my body—head, neck, shoulders, hands and arms, back, chest, stomach, abdomen, legs, and feet.

I am now open to receive the feedback You have for me through my body as I pause for a few minutes.

I am receiving health into every cell of my body through the healing power of Jesus Christ. Thank You, God, for the guidance and the health I receive every day of my life.

Emotional Guidance

Dear God,

Thank You for my emotions. They were woven into the fabric of human creation to give guidance concerning my needs. I ask You now, in Your infinite wisdom, to help me know my true feelings and to learn from them. I know You can help me to deal effectively with my feelings, and to face whatever I need to face. Please help me to get all of my needs met according to Your will of perfect love.

Now I relax my head, neck, shoulders, hands and arms, back, chest, stomach, abdomen, legs, and feet. My mind is relaxed as I place every area of my life in Your care. I am listening, God, for the next few minutes, to what my emotions are, and to what my emotions are telling me.

I am an emotionally healthy, joyful creation of God. Thank You Father, Son, and Holy Spirit for the emotional guidance and health I am receiving today.

Mental Guidance

Dear God,

Thank You for giving me a sound mind. Your Word has instructed me to be transformed by the renewing of my mind. I pray now for that renewal, for a mind open to Your love and guidance. May all of my thoughts be guided and directed by You, recognizing the miracle of my creation and all the beauty and all the gifts with which You created me. I relax my head, neck, shoulders, hands and arms, back, chest, stomach, abdomen, legs, and feet. I relax my mind as I give You my health, my emotions, my spirit, my work, my relationships, my finances, my goals, my future—my all. My life is Yours, God, to do with what You will.

Please direct my thoughts as I wait here for the next few minutes.

I am a child of God. I am loved. I am filled with God's love. Thank You, God, for my transformation, and the renewing of my mind.

Spiritual Guidance

Dear God,

I praise You, God, for Your perfect love which casts out fear, guilt, and resentment, and meets all my needs. Please fill me to overflowing with Your love, so that I may draw closer to You and help meet the needs of others. I open myself to You, God, to fill my body, mind, and spirit with Your love and peace.

I am filled with Your love and peace in my head, neck, shoulders, arms, hands, back, chest, stomach, abdomen, legs, and feet. My mind is focused on Your attributes of love, forgiveness, peace, patience, kindness, power, wisdom, insight, and beauty. I thank You for all the blessings in my life and all the things that are now working together for good in my life.

I praise You, God! And I dwell now on my praise to You.

I am open, God, for Your guidance and direction . . . Your perfect will for my life at this time. I wait for Your words to me. Thank you, God the Father, the Son, and the Holy Spirit, for Your presence in, and guidance of, my life.

Forgiveness

Dear God of all love and forgiveness,

I seek to forgive and be forgiven today. I am open to Your power of forgiveness, now. My will is to forgive all those for whom I have held resentment, regardless of the hurt that came to me from their actions or inactions.

I acknowledge my shortcomings and the ways in which my own action or inaction brought hurt to others.

I relax my body in Your presence, my head, neck, shoulders, arms, hands, back, chest, stomach, abdomen, legs, and feet. Please help me now to recall any people I need to forgive, and as I do that, I make a commitment before You to forgive each through Your perfect love. And please forgive me for holding resentment toward each person.

Please help me to recall any people whose forgiveness I need to ask, whether living or not. For those I need to ask directly, please give me boldness to do so. For those I do not ask directly, let me ask their forgiveness symbolically, as I recall those people in my mind during this prayer.

Thank You, God, that I am free!

LOOKING
FOR LOVE
IN ALL THE
RIGHT PLACES

Supportive people listen. They prove they're listening by asking questions and making relevant comments about what you are saying. Supportive people are genuinely interested in you but rarely give advice and never judge you. They respect your intelligence enough to let you make important decisions for yourself. Supportive people do more than listen; they share their feelings and ideas with you.

It is helpful to look for a person who has actually worked through significant problems. People who have not had significant losses, stresses, or traumas can be loving and supportive, but they will have a difficult time truly understanding you if you go through significant crisis.

Another trait I like in a supportive person is a sense of humor. The last thing on earth I want is to be around and relying on a person who laughs at my pain; but I also don't want someone who is serious when it's time to say, "We might as well laugh about it!" A well-balanced person can see both the serious and humorous sides of an issue. This is a lot to ask of your support person, but it's a nice trait to have.

These are the most essential characteristics of a person who is capable and willing to be supportive of you in your attempts to get your psychological/emotional needs met.

Where to find these wonderful, rare people is something that everyone would like to know. They are not plentiful, but they are out there. The best advice I've ever heard along this line is to hang out in places where your interests lie. However, most any recreational, educational, spiritual, musical, etc., interests can lead you to places where you will meet and attract supportive people.

HOW TO DEVELOP
A NEW
BELIEF SYSTEM

Y ou want to develop beliefs that are consistent with God's will. Micky Stephens told me she overcame her extreme shyness as an adult when she reasoned, "I am a creation of God. When I belittle myself, I belittle God. I am going to give God credit for creating something wonderful—me!" This was the beginning of Micky's new belief system.

Here are some guidelines for developing new beliefs about yourself which are in line with God's will. Use the following truths to guide you in the process:

I am created in God's image.
I am created for a purpose.
God loves and accepts me, as I am.
God wants me to be healthy, happy, and fulfilled.
God can work miracles in and through my life.
I can trust God *completely.*
I can do all things through Christ.
God is in control of my life; therefore, I can relax!

Begin to look for the positive characteristics you already display, even part of the time. Look for any positive attributes you have a tendency to downplay. Focus on your strengths; they will help you overcome your weaknesses. Success is built upon success, not on struggling with your faults.

1. Make a list of all your positive attributes.
2. Make a statement about yourself based on each one of those qualities.
3. List your perceived shortcomings and failures.
4. Write statements beside each of those, indicating God's love and acceptance of you. Then write statements indicating your love and acceptance of yourself.

5. Write down some attributes you would like to develop in yourself.
6. Write down some goals for your life.
7. Make some statements about how you propose to accomplish these goals.

This process might take you several days or even weeks to compete. You might revise parts of this process from time to time. The important thing is to be diligent in the process. As soon as you have completed these steps, you are ready to establish new beliefs about yourself that will lead you to a new life.

You might also need to establish new beliefs about life in general. Many of the things we were taught about the world are false or incomplete. We tend to think that certain unchangeable laws rule the world and accordingly confine ourselves to living within narrow boundaries when we could be experiencing much more freedom and potential. (What if no one had ever tried to live outside the law of gravity?)

See what beliefs you hold about life that might be limiting you. Try to see the world as a place with infinite possibilities.

What are you doing or not doing just because of *the way things are*? One of the ways we find clarity in life is by opening our minds to new possibilities. Open up to new possibilities in yourself, in life, and in the world.

Ensuring Your Success

There are many people who make wonderful starts at changing their lives for the better. They practice a new self-help plan, a new philosophy, or a new religion with great zeal for a while, but they soon declare it doesn't work. People tend to give up too quickly. That is the only reason new belief systems fail to make a difference. People are inconsistent about practicing them, and then give up trying when they don't see immediate results.

Your new belief system will take time to make lasting changes in your life. Most of your old beliefs have had a lifetime to become established. The new beliefs will be fighting for position.

You might feel you are lying to yourself when you make certain positive statements about yourself, but you must be persistent with these statements. You will eventually believe them and witness dramatic changes in your life. You will think much more clearly, because you will be thinking the truth.

Write three to six statements about yourself that you want to be part of your belief system, such as "I am capable." Have these statements handy whenever you need a boost. Repeat them at least every morning and every night. You might want to revise these statements occasionally. Just be *persistent!*

You might have some old beliefs which are extremely resistant to change. In cases of severe childhood abuse and trauma, there can be beliefs which must be consciously fought for a lifetime. As long as you fight them, they cannot take over again. As long as you rehearse them, your new beliefs will still have a positive effect on your life.

Setting aside rehearsal time is a way of ensuring that your new beliefs will be effective. You can even use time that was formerly useless, like when you're stuck at a traffic light or waiting in line. Instead of dwelling on how irritating the situation is, think about the statements you want to become part of your belief system. The time will go by faster and you will be much closer to your goals!

Another way to deepen your new beliefs is to picture them making the difference you want in your life. See yourself as confident, joyful, successful, loving, generous, and so on. By doing this regularly, your beliefs will become much stronger, much faster.

The second part of the success formula for being the person you want to be is having a relationship with someone who believes in you. This will be your closest support person. There will be plenty of people who show up in your life to discourage you from believing the best about yourself. That is why you need someone to whom you can go for a "reality check." Many of my clients are people who come in just to see if they are on the right track concerning what they believe as opposed to what everyone else is telling them. I am always having to talk people back into believing what is true about themselves because there are so many people who try to recruit others to support their own negative views. It really upsets some people to see a friend, spouse, or co-worker becoming a positive, confident person. Find someone who will help you stick to the positives—the truth—about yourself.

DEFINITION OF A LOVING ATTITUDE

Love begins with an attitude. Few people would profess to being unloving individuals. But how many people actually demonstrate the qualities of love in all of their relationships? The beautiful, polite, charming, friendly person is easy to love. Even a weak, dependent person who really "needs" you is easy to love—so long as he or she goes along with *your* curriculum and doesn't surpass you in knowledge.

If you have a loving attitude, you want whatever is best for another person's growth and development, regardless of how that might affect your relationship. What is best for another person's growth and development might include your being more involved in that person's life, even though you don't think he or she will necessarily enhance your image. It might also mean it is time for you to let go of a relationship, to some degree, even though you would greatly feel the loss.

To love is to be vulnerable. When you make the commitment to love someone, no matter how insignificant that person might seem to you, you never know quite what you might be called upon to experience. You may encounter the greatest intimacy—or the greatest sadness—of your life. This is part of the attitude of love: the willingness to be vulnerable and not shrink away from your commitment when sadness rather than rainbows appears on the horizon. We learn about God by working through all our experiences in relationships.

Some advisors tell us to avoid relationships in which we don't feel comfortable. They say we should not associate with people who do not give as much to a relationship as we do. But who is to say how much a person is truly giving? He or she might be giving all he or she has. For example, some people never had loving parents. How will they learn to love if people keep abandoning them because they don't know how to love perfectly?

It takes a lot of strength to love someone who does not seem to be giving as much as you are to a relationship; but you can gain strength from your relationship with God. You can be confident and secure enough to love people who are not overtly lovable.

It is through loving the ordinary human being that we discover the greatest love of all: the divine, dynamic, explosively powerful love of God. In fact, the more difficult a person is to love, the more you need God's power flowing through you. Therefore, the more you seek to love the unlovable, the more you will know and experience God in your life.

How do you develop a loving attitude? Just ask, and you will. It might take longer than you wanted, for we tend to learn best through experience, but you will develop a loving attitude if you seek it. The actions of love will follow. Be patient with yourself; be loving toward yourself.

THE INGREDIENTS OF HEALTHY LOVE

Since God created us in His image, we have the potential to possess many wonderful and amazing qualities. We can be charming, creative, beautiful, wise, intelligent, happy, and many other desirable things. However, we cannot love the way God loves without having the extra dimension of life only God can add by filling us with His Spirit. This divine love enables us to love what is not naturally lovable: criminals, the physically and mentally shattered, enemies, the arrogant, the moody. By seeking to love the naturally unlovable, we are actually seeking God. In finding love in all of our relationships, we are finding the essence of who and what God is.

Openness

Openness is an aspect of love directly involving your individual human will. If you are open in a relationship, you allow your true feelings to be seen. You also stand up for your own values and beliefs, regardless of what others might think. To experience sincere love, you must be free to express yourself. You must also be willing to allow others to express themselves in the same ways.

Openness directly relates to a willingness to be vulnerable. Any time you openly express your feelings, values, and beliefs, you are taking the chance of having them ridiculed or, worse, ignored. Even well-meaning people can be insensitive about how they respond when you express yourself.

You must realize that the rewards of being open in your relationships are much greater than the risks. You will actually develop more self-respect as you express yourself openly and learn to handle criticism. You become stronger every time you handle criticism with confidence and openness. You experience deeper intimacy every time you are open with someone and he or she affirms your feelings, values, and beliefs.

Openness is the secret to enduring intimacy. When you and another person allow your defenses to fall, you experience a feeling of emotional weightlessness. Even if we don't "fall in love" when we drop our defenses, we do draw much closer to the other person and to God.

Defenses are natural. We are not naturally open with everyone we meet. We hide certain feelings and opinions, we avoid certain topics and people, we pretend to like or dislike certain things in order to fit in. That's part of being human. However, the more we drop defenses, the more intimacy we make possible in our lives.

Couples who wonder why they no longer feel intimate need only trace back to the place and time they began putting up their defenses again. One or both of them felt hurt, betrayed, or taken for granted and put up defenses in order to avoid further hurt. Such a couple needs to talk about whatever caused the defenses to go up, forgive each other for any hurt feelings, and ask for support in attempting to feel "safe" with each other again, so openness can be restored. As long as we are open with people, we can love them, and they can love us.

Acceptance

Acceptance is approving of and caring for a person totally, including the person's traits you don't understand.

If we don't accept people, we are likely judging them. Being judgmental is something our greatest example, Christ, said does not exist within principles of love. He said when we judge other people, we become blind to our own faults and are therefore more likely to make mistakes.

In fact the traits we find most intolerable in other people are likely ones we tend to have ourselves. We can hide and be blind to traits we find intolerable. Then when we see those traits in other people, we overreact. You can usually tell the personal traits a person has hidden from himself by noticing what he is most outspoken against. For example, someone with a tendency toward addiction might be very judgmental toward alcoholics or cigarette smokers; yet he would not see that his own obsession with exercise or food is actually a form of addiction.

Another reason we might speak judgmentally is so we can feel superior to others. Every time we criticize another person's behavior or viewpoint, we imply we are superior to that person and don't have any significant faults ourselves.

One way to avoid the folly of being judgmental is to face your own faults squarely. It is okay to have faults. It is part of being human. Accept that fact. Occasionally take a close look at yourself. When you find yourself overreacting to the behaviors and viewpoints of others, see if you have become blind to some tendency in yourself. Face whatever that trait is, accept it as part of your humanity, then ask God to help you refine that trait into something He can use in a positive way in your life. You will find yourself feeling much freer, being much more open, and much more accepting of the differences in others.

If you find yourself repeatedly faced with a type of person or point of view you find difficult, perhaps you need to work on your compassion. God created the diversity and variety in life. Trying to understand each other can bring us closer to understanding God. Compassion fosters a deeper love and a more enriched life.

Life itself is so full of diversity, and nature so full of variety, that we cannot possibly understand everything and everyone. And we must just accept what we cannot understand.

Affirmation

Affirming someone is showing you relate to him or her in some way. You can affirm opinions, values, beliefs, and feelings. Emphasizing the things that you *do* understand will open up communication in a relationship.

Affirming someone while you disagree with him will show that you care even during conflict and it is okay for him to express himself. Affirming someone after she has hurt you will prove you will not reject her even when she makes a mistake. This will cause most people to be less likely to hurt you again. We hurt people through being defensive. If you consistently affirm the other person, he or she will have no reason to be defensive and, therefore, no reason to hurt you.

Forgiveness

Forgiveness is essential to love. Mistakes are inherent in any relationship. Without freely given forgiveness, love would not exist. Most relationships do not become or remain loving because people stop forgiving.

Forgiveness means not holding someone accountable for their behavior that offended you. Once you forgive, you never bring up that offense again. Even in your private thoughts, you do not allow resentment to take root. I am not talking about denial or repression of your feelings. You do not have to forget the offense. You just need to release your anger, resentment, and hurt concerning the offensive behavior.

You can best accomplish this by expressing your feelings to the offender, asking that person to help you forgive him or her, then dropping the issue. The other person can help you forgive by acknowledging his or her error or insensitivity, or by simply apologizing.

Once you have expressed your feelings to the person who offended you, it is your responsibility to forgive. That person may never apologize or acknowledge any wrongdoing, but you can still let go of the grievance. In a truly loving relationship, you forgive unconditionally... no apology necessary.

If you find that you have a difficult time forgiving someone, apology offered or not, talk to someone else about your feelings. First, talk to

God. It is only the love of God working through us that makes us able to forgive. Ask God to forgive that person through you. Counselors or therapists can also help.

Often when we have a difficult time forgiving someone, it is because of someone in our past we have forgotten about. We often hold onto resentments without even being aware of it. This subconscious resentment keeps you from forgiving people in the present, especially if they remind you in some way of people who offended you in the past.

Talk to an insightful, nonjudgmental person about the people who hurt you in the past. Then ask God to help you forgive them. You will find it much easier to deal with the present once you have dealt with the past.

Don't forget to forgive yourself. The resentments we hold against ourselves can be much more damaging than those we hold against other people. If you are hard on yourself, you will be less forgiving toward other people. Be gentle with yourself. Acknowledge your wrongdoing; then, forgive yourself, and accept God's forgiveness.

When you realize that you require forgiveness yourself, you will be much more willing to give it to others.

Patience

Patience implies *waiting* for something to happen. We wait for people to mature, learn, grow, gain insight, overcome a fault, or break a habit. Patience is being nonjudgmental toward people who have not reached a level of functioning in life that we hope for. Patience is also being gentle with people while they work on their lives, in whatever way they choose, at whatever rate of speed they are able. Patience gleans more than prodding.

Kindness

Kindness is an awareness of others, their feelings, their preferences, and their needs. Kindness is *acting on* that awareness by doing things compatible with those feelings, preferences, and needs. There is nothing more pleasurable than being with someone who is tuned in to you and puts you at ease. This is what kindness accomplishes in a relationship.

Peacefulness

Peacefulness exists in loving relationships because of the trust that develops from kindness, forgiveness, affirmation, acceptance, and openness. People who love know what to expect from and are at peace with themselves. Knowing that you are going to be consistently loving with others, even when they are not loving toward you, gives you an edge in life. You can be confident in all situations because you know that you will handle them with the greatest power available to any human: the power of God's love.

The resulting peace is much greater than the peace that comes from having someone else care for your needs, having a big bank account, or having tremendous physical ability. Trusting yourself to turn to God for help in loving others produces self-control and tranquility, which you can use to overcome obstacles, make the most of opportunities, and enjoy to the fullest the blessings that come your way.

The greatest joy you can know comes from being an unconditionally loving person. As long as you are loving in all that you do, you know that only good will ultimately result from all your efforts.

The more you seek God, the more you are able to love. The more you love, the closer you are to God. The closer you are to God, the more joyful you become.

THE DIFFERENCE BETWEEN GIVING LOVE AND TAKING ABUSE

Many people think of a loving person as some kind of wimp who smiles weakly as people use, abuse, and run over him or her. Nothing could be further from the truth. Loving effectively requires a tremendous amount of personal strength and self-respect. You need no strength or personal character to be hostile, resentful, self-pitying, or defensive. The real wimps are those who go with the flow of their hostilities and insecurities by protecting themselves with aggression. Weak people don't even attempt love. They defend themselves in this greatest of all challenges by withdrawing from close relationships or appearing unfriendly.

Strong people overcome the natural insecurities, hurts, and resentments inherent in living in this world. Reaching out to love even a lovable person is difficult, much less an unloving person. One must continually face and overcome personal insecurities and resentments to even begin to love. But loving people accept the challenge and become strong and secure even if it requires the self-exploration of psychotherapy or the discipline of spiritual pursuits.

Loving people develop self-respect. They will not allow anyone to endanger them physically, emotionally, or spiritually. One of the most harmful things you can do is allow another person to behave irresponsibly toward you. By taking abuse, you teach that abusive behavior is okay. You need to confront such behavior any time it happens, continuing to demonstrate love even toward those acting it out. You should never take repeated attacks from a psychologically, emotionally, or physically abusive person. There are some people you need to love from a distance.

You are not unloving if you choose to cut off abusive relationships. Some people enjoy watching others suffer. These people can be helped if they seek God and therapy, but if they don't even try to get help, they will continue to abuse people until there is no one left in their lives. You are actually doing chronically abusive people a favor to insist that they seek help and to love them from a distance until they do.

EXPERIENCING GOD'S AFFECTION

We can experience God's love several ways. One is by applying the attributes of love and treating ourselves with more patience, gentleness, support, affirmation, forgiveness, and encouragement. As you practice these loving attitudes toward yourself, you will become more loving toward other people. You will also attract more love in your life *from* other people. When you have love for yourself, you naturally, unconsciously, give others the impression that you are a person who can accept the love of others. There are many people who would love to love you! Give them the chance!

We can experience the love of God through others. Another way to experience the love of God is to picture Him holding you and telling you how much He loves you. This image will help you to gain more trust in God. Any time you feel the need to experience more love, close your eyes for a few minutes, relax, and see God loving you. The more you do this, the more easily you will love others and the easier it will be to listen to what God has to say to you.

Picturing yourself being loved by God is an excellent therapeutic exercise, especially for those who were under-loved or abused as children. For people who received inadequate or harmful demonstrations of parental affection, there is a frightened, suspicious child inside. This "child" part of our personal makeup responds very favorably to imagination. Children use imagination extensively and effectively in the development of their personalities and their ideas about life. This developmental process and these ideas about life affect us profoundly throughout adulthood. Since we are all part-child, we can use our imaginations as a healing experience, especially to heal the hurts of childhood.

The Twenty-third Psalm is an illustration of God's love to us. As you read it out loud, see in your mind all of the ways God demonstrates love to you.

"The LORD is my shepherd; / I shall not want," means all of your needs are met in a relationship with God. See yourself with all of your needs met.

"He makes me to lie down in green pastures; / He leads me beside the still waters. / He restores my soul," means that God gives comfort, rest, and renewed life to our spirits when we turn to Him. Picture God filling you with new vitality.

"He leads me in the paths of righteousness / For His name's sake," means that God will lead us to do what is right, good, and in keeping with His perfect will for us. Just ask God for that guidance. Then trust that you are receiving it.

"Yea, though I walk through the valley of the shadow of death, / I will fear no evil; / For You are with me; / Your rod and Your staff, they comfort me," means that God's guidance will get us through even the most evil, threatening situations in our lives. See God giving you protection and guidance in the situations of life you most fear. Soon, those will no longer *be* fears.

"You prepare a table before me in the presence of my enemies," describes how God can help us confidently face even our enemies, and go beyond merely facing them, to actually sitting down with them in the peacefulness and intimacy of a meal. Imagine you and the people who seem to be against you sitting down together and feasting in peace and harmony.

"You anoint my head with oil," is a depiction of God performing the ancient healing ritual of placing drops of oil on the forehead of the person who is seeking healing. See God giving you a healing touch. Experience the feeling of healing in your body.

"My cup runs over," is a symbol of the abundant prosperity which God wants all of us to receive. Imagine God supplying for all of your needs, abundantly.

"Surely goodness and mercy shall follow me / All the days of my life; / And I will dwell in the house of the LORD / Forever," affirms the fact that God wants us to accept His goodness and mercy every day of our lives. Make that statement of affirmation and acceptance. You will experience more and more of God's goodness and mercy.

NOTES

Chapter 1: The Common Sense Feedback of the Body

1. From a live personal interview with O. Carl Simonton, M.D., during which he discussed the principles outlined in his book *Getting Well Again* with Stephanie Matthews-Simonton and James L. Creighton (New York: Bantam, 1978).

Chapter 2: The Common Sense Feedback of the Emotions

1. The eight psychological needs listed were adapted from and used by permission of

Dr. Taibi Kahler, *The Mastery of Management* (Little Rock: Kahler Communications, 1988).
2. Friedrich Wilhelm Nietzsche, 1844-1900.
3. Victor E. Frankl, *Man's Search for Meaning* (Boston: Beacon Press, 1984), 115.

Chapter 5: The Ultimate Source of Guidance

1. Dr. Elaine Hatfield, *Los Angeles Times*, 8 November 1991.

Chapter 7: Discerning God's Voice

1. "Know Who You Are," words and music by Roger Hodgson and Rick Davies, copyright © 1981 by Delicate Music. Almo Music Corp. administers for Delicate Music for the World. All Rights Reserved. International Copyright Secured. Used by permission.

ABOUT THE AUTHOR

C. CHRISTOPHER KNIPPERS, Ph.D., is director of Capistrano Community Christian Counseling Services in San Juan Capistrano, California. A psychotherapist and counselor for more than eighteen years, Dr. Knippers earned a doctorate in Clinical Psychology at the California School of Professional Psychology in Fresno, California. He also serves as assistant pastor with the Rev. Robert A. Schuller at Rancho Capistrano Community Church in San Juan Capistrano, California.

Dr. Knippers is a popular speaker and has written articles for *On the Homefront*, a newsletter for U.S. troops in the Persian Gulf, and *RE News*, published by Rancho Capistrano Renewal Center, Robert Schuller Ministries. He lives in Laguna Niguel, California.

To contact Dr. Knippers for a speaking engagement you may write to him at:

P. O. Box 358
San Juan Capistrano, CA 92675